for Rachel, Harper, and Jesse

First published in the United Kingdom in 2023 by Brand Nu, brandnubooks.co.uk

Mindful Creative - How to *understand* and deal with the highs and lows of *creative* life, career and business

Copyright ©2023 Radim Malinic

1

The right of Radim Malinic to be identified as author of this work has been asserted by him in accordance with the Copyright, Design and Patent Act 1988.

Written by Radim Malinic

Editor Shaun Patrick Hand

Cover illustration Timo Kuilder

Illustrator Emily Melling

Breathing exercises Adiba Osmani

Proofreader Gemma Rowlands

Proofreader Shelby Jones

Creative direction + design Radim Malinic

British Library Cataloguing-in-Publication Data A catalogue record for this book is available from the British Library

Made in London, England

Printed by Park Communications on FSC® certified paper. Park works to the EMAS standard and its Environmental Management System is certified to ISO 14001.

This publication has been manufactured using 100% offshore wind electricity sourced from UK wind.

100% of the inks used are vegetable oil based, 95% of press chemicals are recycled for further use and, on average 99% of any waste associated with this production will be recycled and the remaining 1% used to generate energy.

This book is printed on Edixion Offset paper made of material from well-managed, FSC®-certified forests and other controlled sources.

This is a certified climate neutral print product for which carbon emissions have been calculated and offset by supporting recognised carbon offset projects. The carbon offset projects are audited and certified according to international standards and demonstrably reduce emissions.

The climate neutral label includes a unique ID number specific to this product which can be tracked at climatepartner.com, giving details of the carbon offsetting process including information on the emissions volume and the carbon offset project being supported.

To find out more about this publication or the author, visit **radimmalinic.co.uk** or **brandnubooks.co.uk**

ISBN 978-0-9935400-5-9 [paperback]

Also available as ebook and audiobook

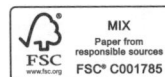

Carbon neutral
Print product
ClimatePartner.com/13766-2309-1003

MIX
Paper from
responsible sources
FSC
www.fsc.org
FSC® C001785

Mindful Creative

How to *understand* and <u>deal</u> with
the **highs** and **lows** of *creative*
life, **career** and **business**

Radim Malinic

Brand Nu®

Contents

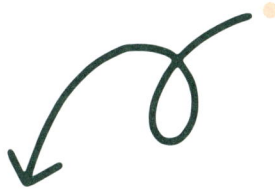

Creativity nearly killed me

It was 4 a.m. on a Wednesday morning. I lit a cigarette standing in the backyard of my basement apartment in south-west London. It was a warm summer morning, and the world around me was still dreaming. The glow of my cigarette signalled the end of another day's work — I'd been grafting for nearly 16 hours. Despite the long haul and late finish, I felt ready to continue for another few hours if need be. It had been yet another marathon session in the office, fuelled by a mixture of caffeine, nicotine, adrenaline, and dopamine, but I didn't mind; I was fully devoted to my work, my deadlines, and my clients.

Finishing my smoke, I checked my emails one last time and re-checked the piece of work I'd just finished. I also looked over my to-do list for the coming day, which would be starting a mere five or six hours hence. 'Tomorrow' would likely be another long one: meetings, client calls across different time-zones, feedback sessions, work promotion, folio tweaking, and learning. I'd get up mid-morning to look after the admin, reserving the creative work for the evening, when the world became quieter and I could focus. Technically, I would work two eight-hour days, only in one calendar day.

New business was coming in from all angles, and any spare moments were filled with self-initiated learning. I believed I was in love with what I was doing, but 'obsessed' is more accurate. Nothing seemed amiss, though; I was the main man, the one keeping the plates spinning.

I had no idea of how addicted I was. If anything, I wore my 'work ethic' as a badge of honour — it became my identity. Every day, I was chasing the next high, just like any other addict. From getting enquiries, to doing the work, submitting it, and getting paid, each step felt crucial to my sense of worth. Having been in demand ever since deciding to set up on my own, I'd never paused to reflect on how far I'd come or what issues I might need to address.

My actions and emotions were underpinned by the search for security that came with running my own business. There was no fall-back or warehouse of stock ready to ship. Each new piece of work was a blank canvas: new clients, new briefs, new obstacles. If the work dried up, my bank balance would do the same; I had no safety net. I was growing a business as an emigre from a different country in a city that I now called home.

Projects came with diverse requirements and overlapping deadlines, all of which I felt equal to. There was no routine, no long-term plan; it was a punishing cycle of go-go-go and the perfect recipe for chaos, but somehow it worked. Just.

You'd be forgiven for thinking that I was doing all this to build some sort of multi-million-pound business empire. How else does one justify so enthusiastically making themselves ill? Indeed, such reckless behaviour is generally reserved for high-earners whose job titles come with high demands; but there I was with my three titles (Art Director + Designer + Illustrator) splashed across my website, working away in my apartment, doing all I could to ensure the wheel kept turning, my clients were as happy as possible, and that I remained focused on producing exponentially better work.

The incoming commissions included many high-profile advertising campaigns, work for internationally renowned brands, and dozens and dozens of other projects. The highs were super high and the work was engaging. It seemed like the best feeling ever. I bought it all, without seeing the high price tag.

Only after sprinting on this treadmill for many years did I realise that my superpowers were waning. The caffeine and adrenalin could only do so much to keep me awake. My circadian rhythm was shot. I was going to bed as the world woke up, and getting up by the time it reached its first coffee break.

I was both over-caffeinated and severely dehydrated. I smoked too many cigarettes. On many occasions when I socialised, I would drink too much too quickly, which never goes well. My idea of exercise was the odd session on a static bike in the corner of my apartment. I thought that I could maximise every minute of every day for work, which meant not going out unless I had to — a brisk walk to the Tube station was my lot. I reasoned that I could balance all the bad stuff with a decent diet (which I just about managed to stick to). And just like every broken person, I believed that everything was fine. I worked it out recently, and in my first 20 years of running my own creative business, I put in 30 years' worth of hours. Don't try it at home.

My mental health was deteriorating, but I ploughed on. Even when I spent one of my birthdays crying into a slice of cake, utterly exhausted, no alarm bells rang and nothing changed. The remorseless grind kept me on course for the cliff-edge.

I'm lucky to have survived that part of my life without any serious long-term damage. Of course, there were fuck-ups and blackouts aplenty, but I emerged the other side with all four limbs intact and all five senses working.

And you know what? It was all my choice. The title of this introduction is, perhaps, unfair. Creativity didn't nearly kill me; I nearly killed me. I made all the wrong decisions, I bought into the wrong mindset and beliefs. I can't deny that doing so opened many doors for me, but I've long since realised that there could have been a far better way of doing it.

A creative career can take enough out of you as it is; you don't need to make it worse for yourself. With no set plan beyond ensuring the bills are covered every month, we often have no defined expectations, or even defined successes — we don't know our 'enough'. I sure as hell didn't know mine. It took me at least 10 years to work out there even was such a thing. Life and work were both coming at me full-pelt, and I was happily opening my arms to catch as much as I could. Until the moment I suddenly couldn't anymore.

Thankfully, more than a decade ago, the turning point came: my knight in shining armour turned out to be a girl called Rachel on an ex-racehorse called Sean. Both utter legends. Much like me, Sean was a bundle of chaos, and it took Rachel a good few years to make us both listen to her wisdom and stop making fools of ourselves.

Rachel and I are now married and the proud parents of two young children who are hard at work on their potential comedy careers. At least I think that's what they're doing. It's so easy to get side-tracked and end up in something like chaos again, but for at least a decade now, I've been working to form the right habits, follow healthy routines, and act on the knowledge that I continue to find along the way, but through all of that, I am still a work in progress and always will be. Hopefully, compiling and sharing what I know about the beast of creativity will help others avoid making the same mistakes I did. Doing so feels not only right but also necessary.

If you feel thirsty, you're already dehydrated; if you need help with mental health, you're already in trouble. The key is to anchor yourself so you don't end up drifting further from the shore than necessary and this book is all about it.

I still love creativity; it changed my life — but it nearly broke me for good too. It's a beautiful beast, but we have to learn how to tame it.

So let's get started

Preface

If you're trying to decide whether this book is for you, then let me give you a quick overview of its contents. This is a book about how not to let having a creative career in the 21st century ruin your life. Your individual creativity is a gift, something to be nurtured and enjoyed. It should enrich your life, not harm it.

This book will be valuable whether you're already earning your living from creative pursuits or still at the planning stage. If you feel like you're trapped in a circle of overwork, stress, and burnout, then it is definitely for you. However, it's important to state from the off that none of the advice contained here is intended as therapy or medical advice for any mental or physical health issues you may be suffering. I am neither a qualified medical professional nor a licensed therapist. If you need assistance with any problems in those areas, then I urge you to seek professional help. Similarly, if any of the breathing exercises described cause discomfort, please stop doing them immediately.

What the advice here can do is, hopefully, be the nudge you need towards building a healthier creative lifestyle.

This book is divided into two halves: the first deals with the person we creatives see in the mirror: what drives us, what upends us, and how we can audit our lives to stop ourselves from burning out (again). The second half is proactive, outlining practical self-care methods that can help to keep us balanced as we progress on our creative journey.

Here's a little more information on each section:

Creativity vs Human

From page 18

The first section examines what it means to be a creative human in the first half of the 21st century. This includes how our increased connectivity to others and the abundance of information we're now bombarded with as a matter of course can both help and harm our expectations. It also considers how making our creativity our work can affect our relationship with it

From page 46

Mind Full

We then take a look at the different kinds of issues that can overwhelm us in our day-to-day lives and turn what we thought might be a smooth ride into a jolting rollercoaster. Everything from a lack of presence in our own minds, to pointless distractions, Imposter Syndrome, outside criticism, and even the emergence of AI are considered here

From page 72

Pause

We can't make any meaningful changes to our lives or work if we carry on with business as usual, falling into the same unhelpful grooves over and over again. This section considers life and work together and encourages you to make time to reflect on both how far you've come and what might need changing — you can't fix a leaky pipe if you don't know where the water's coming from

From page 90

Define

This is perhaps my favourite section of the book. It challenges you to define various aspects of yourself through honest reflection — who you are, how you are, what you want to achieve, what's holding you back, and who's there to support you. This is the closest that you come in this book to carrying out a life audit.

Help From page 110

The title of this section is self-explanatory. As we look after physical health, and even our material possessions, so we should take care of our minds. Here, I share some of my experiences with various forms of therapy and why I strongly advocate for seeking the right professional help for you.

Mindful

From page 132

From here on, the book becomes more proactive. In this section, we look ahead and start implementing small but essential steps to take us from mind full to mindful. Small changes can give rise to long-term impacts, and we explore how finding ways to simply be can help you respond calmly to any given situation. This section includes instructions for some simple breathing exercises, body scans, and meditations.

Positive Habits
From page 164

The seventh section builds on the previous two, encouraging you to build and maintain positive habits that will help you as you work towards your goal. It encourages you to adopt a balanced, manageable workload and lifestyle and gives you practical tips on how to not let things slip

From page 186 ## Flow States

The penultimate section looks towards the point where everything is hopefully coming to fruition — the pieces of the puzzle should start forming a new picture. It takes a close look at 'flow states' — those magical times when we become one with our work and realise the full extent of our creative potential. It also explains how to create the optimal conditions to achieve such states

See page 204 ## Grow

For every mountain you successfully scale, more will remain in front of you. If the muscle of resilience isn't kept trained, it will soon turn flabby, and all those old habits will come flooding back. The final section of this book gives you advice on how to keep showing up, and tackle each new mountain as it appears

pages

18 —— 45

Chapter - no.1

Creativity ^{vs} Human

Chapter - no.1

36. When the play becomes the income

38. *The escape: a shortcut to instant gratification*

40. Creativity in the 21st century

42. *Meeting the untamed beast — too many choices, lack of rules?*

43. Creativity is an eternal lesson in growing resilience

Creativity starts with a blank piece of paper

It's almost impossible to define exactly what creativity means to us — that's part of its magic. We could list verbs for every letter of the alphabet to describe it, and we still wouldn't quite capture it. It can amaze us, bedevil us, chase us, define us, elude us, frustrate us. Sometimes it seems to use us as much as we use it.

But however we think about creativity, if we go right back to the beginning, we will always find the same thing: a blank piece of paper. It might be physical; it might be on a screen. But it's there. And there's nothing on it. Yet.

There's something both unnerving and exhilarating about that blank page in front of you. You can be stuck one minute and on your way to greatness mere seconds later. The page silently witnesses those moments, which can change fortunes, futures, and even lives. It's the arena for idea origination and mind-maps; the canvas for doodles and sketches; the initial setting of every story ever written; bearing witness to expressive words turning into timeless poetry, or the site where visual thinkers can experiment with shape and form.

At least, that's the plan.

The creative process can be hard; it's not meant to be easy. If it was, we wouldn't keep going back for more. We would lose interest very quickly. Imagine getting answers to your creative conundrums at the click of a button — a world where you could simply press P on your keyboard and get a poster, I for illustration, W for website; all the work done for you. M for Masterpiece. H for Happiness. WTF for... I will let you fill that blank.

The prospect of ready-made answers appears most compelling when we hit a creative roadblock. Being stuck in a dead-end hits the hardest, especially at the beginning of our journey, before we've accumulated enough experience to find answers. It's times like that when you might consider throwing in the towel, and hurling your laptop across the room for good measure, screaming, *"Why did no one tell me it would be this £*#%ing hard?!"*

Yep, the blank piece of paper definitely witnesses some challenging times and a fair bit of despair. But with perseverance, the creative process does start to make sense, and the aim of these pages is to offer you tools to help you create that process for yourself, within the context of being a human in the 21st century.

When creativity works, it can be the best feeling in the world. When the sketch turns into a finished piece. When chords start forming a tune. When words start forming a captivating story. It genuinely can feel like the greatest choice you've ever made in your life.

But unlocking that creativity rarely happens by accident.

To be able to turn a blank piece of paper into the next big idea, day in, day out, requires patience, experience, and accumulative skills and knowledge. This is the boxing ring where long-term careers are made or terminated — think of all the aches and bruises that come from pushing through those tough times when idea after idea refuses to work, when you're trying to bend, punch, or ram something into shape, and all to no avail.

Creativity is the fuel that helps us make the invisible visible, over and over again. Options to turbocharge it are plentiful — everything from books, creative software, and tutorials how to use them all the way to emerging new technologies — but one thing is guaranteed: physical or digital, the blank page will always be the clearest starting point. We need the uneasy and exhilarating because we're hardwired for constant problem-solving; we need some form of struggle to keep us on our toes and help us grow. Even though we love to dream about easy processes and effortless creativity

The highway of life and creativity

Picture yourself driving a car along a highway. You're following the speed of the other vehicles and sharing the same few lanes designated for travel at different momentums. The view ahead isn't expansive; not much beyond a few cars in front. In free-flowing traffic, that's enough; you don't need to see miles ahead. The presence of other vehicles moving forward in the same fashion as yours is reassurance enough that the way forward is clear and ultimately safe. Everyone is moving in unison on their journey.

But accidents do happen, and they can happen in a split second, right in front of our eyes. Even worse, we can be in the crash. Worse still, it can be our fault.

Shit happens. As much as we tell ourselves that all sorts of dangers can be avoided or even prevented, once we join the highway, we are in the mix with everyone else, exposed to outside factors that change probability ratios across different metrics and scenarios — it's more likely accidents will happen.

But witnessing a bad crash doesn't always encourage drivers to be on their best behaviour, even if they narrowly avoid being involved themselves. Optimism bias, the tendency we humans have to invent our own, highly subjective reality, can often keep us believing that a) nothing truly terrible can ever happen to us and b) we're better than other people at stuff. We think we drive better than others; we think we care more than others; *we think we're more creative than others.*

Such bias makes it surprisingly easy for us to convince ourselves that the odds are stacked in our favour, that we're over-performing over-achievers, that we're practically invincible. Sure, there may be bumps along the way, but they're only momentary blips on an otherwise steady road. Yet it's important that we check our objective realities and fortunes and reflect on how our actions can affect other people and their realities and fortunes. No creative career happens in a vacuum. No life doesn't overlap with others. We all overlap around the edges of our lives. We are connected and we need each other, but it's a truth that we often deny. We are all on the highway of life, driving towards something we're striving for. We can be reassured by the presence of others that our actions are most likely the correct ones. What we're doing at least seems to resemble what others are doing around us.

Or does it?

Society has recalibrated the need for speed as a major metric for success, fortune, and even happiness. The faster you're moving, the more admiration and rewards are assumed to follow. Those in the inside lanes whose speedometer readings, however much lower, hold greater personal value, and whose journeys are potentially more enriching (and maybe even a little safer), can often be perceived as lacking ambition. They aren't big, bold, or strong; they're second-rate.

If you want to pursue other routes and encounter some unique journey, then headless ambitious speed freaks may well look at you with such bewilderment that you begin questioning your decisions. They will do all they can to convince you that all the good stuff only happens where they are — and the bigger the city, the better and faster the life. After all, size matters, right?

Ultimately, at a certain level, we are all equal. Some of us are content with where we are; some of us will be searching for a long time to come. The latter often draw the most attention because they make the loudest noise. They rush in all directions to get somewhere, without ever knowing where that somewhere is. They're the white rabbit from *Alice's Adventures in Wonderland*, but without a party to head for.

Staying on the quest and forever moving forwards offers protection from uncomfortable thoughts of slowing down, and God forbid, stopping for a moment

Tuning into the right channels

If it's easy to paint our chances in a positive light, then it's even easier to buy into the success mindset that is sold to us every day. If you were to take a snapshot of the mainstream media — print, TV, and digital — and less-gatekept, user-generated content, then you'd see how much of it is populated with messaging likely to make us feel anxious, stressed, and underachieving. Every other YouTube video seems to be prefaced by an advert starring a self-certified millionaire trying to hard sell you their money-making course. When you want to catch up on the latest tweets, you'll quickly be bombarded with people boasting about their material wealth or their moral brilliance. As fast as you can blink, you'll be informed that you need to do more, better, faster. You need to upscale your skillsets to make your first million, because alongside speed, another major metric of success, creativity, and happiness is, of course, money.

These kinds of messages can be best described as 'money porn' and 'success porn': pornographic because they present a make-believe world filled with hyper-realistic images of intimacy — an over-processed reality. Now, however, we also have 'creative porn'. Mass portfolio websites are the height of this phenomena, and rather than excite or encourage you, they too can make you feel hopelessly inadequate. You can see what projects you can't do and have no chance of winning; you can see how much smaller your brand is, and how you don't have any big-name trophy clients to list on your homepage.

If we feel excited and hopeful when we first open our browser, then it can take mere minutes of browsing to make us feel the polar opposite.

But only if we allow it.

It's natural to want to join in, to weave your way over to the fast lane as quickly as possible. But it's a toxic race to a perpetual horizon that ultimately works against its own, admittedly vague ends: endless days and nights of work, stress, and even blind panic to gather as much forward momentum as possible. Without realising the implications, your diary and workload grow in size and weight. What began as an exciting journey towards freedom can soon feel like dragging a boulder up a mountain. Things can get beyond your control. Yes, you're only doing what others have done to gain success, but are you doing it right? More importantly, is it right for you? When we dive down that rabbit hole, following the aimless white rabbit, are we aware of the reality, quickly zooming out of the gloom to meet us, that we are not, in fact, invincible?

Self-inflicted high workload and an equally self-inflicted muddle of deadlines can do a great job of clouding our judgement and stealing our precious energy and resilience. Like success and money, creativity can be addictive, especially when we attach our deep anxieties, hopes, and fears to agents that allow us to lose sight of what we are here to be, make, or fix.

Aware of the solution. In denial of the facts.

Our uber-connected worlds love to take a piece of information and make it go viral: a throwaway piece of content that will be forgotten as quickly as it appeared. And honestly, this is best for all concerned. TikToks of cute cats don't need to be elevated to the same status as *The Godfather II*; it's enough to glance them as they whizz across our consciousness and disappear. Such content is another piece of 'porn': hyper-realistic entertainment that stimulates our dopamine receptors in small doses. It doesn't involve spending time getting to understand a much bigger piece of storytelling, with ultimately larger conclusions and rewards for the time we've invested.

Time is our currency, but we spend it unwisely, every hour of every day. Worse, this is something we can't solely blame ourselves for — and it's worse because something that isn't our fault is harder to change. Legions of 'attention engineers' have pored over research findings exploring the parts of our ancestral minds that respond to short-term thinking and rewards. It's no conspiracy to state that the companies force-feeding us seemingly trivial content know how to engage our brains and keep us scrolling. If they didn't, they wouldn't have businesses with billions of users.

Our thoughts and desires are often preoccupied with the possible future outcomes of our actions in the present moment, yet we spend said moment engaging with elements that ultimately incinerate any positive future outcome. The irony is, however, that among the melee of micro-content, messages, and short videos often exists a small amount of valuable information that can unlock a positive change in someone. It could be something that has been in plain sight forever, but which needed unlocking by a third party.

We share more information than ever — and that includes more valuable information than ever. As a society, we know more about ourselves and each other than at any point in history, and we know how to do and make things better than any society ever has. Yet we struggle more than ever before, too. We like saying stuff. A lot of stuff. Yet we don't always pay enough attention to what we should be hearing. We might pay rapt attention to a motivational speaker, or give ourselves endless amounts of pep talks, but still nothing changes.

Even when we're aware of an impending crash, we don't often do much to avoid it. No matter how many warning signs we see or read motivational quotes on the very issue, we still play down what's about to happen to us.

Being aware of the solution often doesn't make us face up to the facts.

All of this is part of our evolution, or lack of it, both societal and personal. For all of our sophistication, mistakes are being repeated across the ages, generation after generation. Technological advancements and innovative progress are accelerating, yet we're still grappling with basic concepts that have been known to us for thousands of years. We can share our thoughts with thousands of strangers almost instantaneously, but we can still find it hard to take just 30 seconds to sit still and appraise how we're actually feeling, let alone accept and do something about how we're actually feeling.

The biggest gift you can give yourself is to watch for the signs that could take you off-course. They are often easy to spot, but hard to avoid. If you become aware of the possibility of impending doom, do something about it so it never materialises. Slow down. Change lanes. Pull over and ask for help. Make yourself familiar with solutions that can positively influence your current issues and problems. Our journeys are littered with experiences that make us feel either 10-feet tall or show us just how deep rock bottom is, and there is something important to be taken from all of them.

It's not meant to be easy, but it's not meant to be impossible.

Keeping the scales balanced (part 1)

If you don't water a plant enough, it will die. If you water it too much, you'll deprive its root of oxygen, and it too will die. The plant needs just enough every so often to stay alive, flourish, and keep growing. And just like a flower needs water, your creativity needs time and space. Both are a part of your nature. They need looking after to stay alive, flourish, and keep evolving.

Each of us has a unique relationship with creativity. We all have it in us, and although some couldn't care less about it, others will despair if anything keeps them from getting lost in their deeply personal world. If you're reading this book, I'm assuming you're with me in the latter group. We're always opening doors and lifting lids to see what others are doing and how it can influence or improve what we're doing. Our eternal curiosity is part of the magic formula that keeps the world moving forward — and it's an essential part of the magic formula that makes us who we are.

But, for a creative soul, it can often feel like endless obstacles, aka life, get in the way. If we don't feel the time is right, we don't have the space or energy to explore our ideas, or we can't put them into action, our excitement can turn to frustration in no time. Our childlike impulses kick in. Switch off your child's TV programme and watch their reaction. They won't be happy, and they'll be super quick to let you know. I'm sure you've felt the same as an adult when a creative avenue has suddenly been closed to you.

Similarly, if you show a child a new toy or game, they'll instantly want to try it and won't want to stop anytime soon. As we grow older and start acting like boring grown-ups with mortgages and bills to pay, any opportunity to 'play' can become a direct teleport to similar emotions and sensations. The chemical reactions in our minds and bodies are direct results of making something new and exciting. We start to want to do more. We expect to do more. We throw a tantrum if we can't do it right here, right now.

Give a creative a few small projects, and we'll soon strive for more. We'll grow our skillset and understanding. We'll take on more work and the admin that comes with it. We'll balance it all and take on even more without asking for any help or thought of delegation. We're very good at making people believe we can do it all. But then the scales tip over to the other side, the heavy side, and our superpowers start to fade.

Creative overload is a thing. It can kill off excitement, energy, and even long-term vision. Balancing the scales can become a career-long exercise that is often led by the elements, not us.

When a genius idea strikes, it seldom does so at the right place or time — there's always some sort of life or work admin task in the way. And that's kind of why the best ideas appear when we're on top of a mountain or in the shower; our minds are freed for a moment. It just so happens that these are also the times we're least likely to have the means to jot the idea down. And what about if you happen to have an exciting new idea whilst in the middle of creating something else? Do you see the existing one through to completion or immediately make the other a priority? Such are the general woes of millions of creatives around the world who follow their heart and soul by expressing their ideas through creative work. It begs the question: is there ever a right time for creativity?

To those outside the creative sphere, this can all appear as one big precious, self-indulgent headache: "So you have it, and you can do it, but not at the right time, or there's not enough time, or it's not the right place. You want to do more, but when you get more, it's overwhelming? Pick a lane!"

Of course, similar issues can be found anywhere — and people in non-creative jobs are increasingly finding their workload becoming a work overload as more and more is expected of them, but this book is for and about creative humans, so let's continue to dig a little deeper into what it means to be a creative and a human being in the 21st century, battling the elements to create the optimal conditions for growth

Being creative vs. creative expectations

Creativity comes in an endless supply. It's a gift. From the earliest sensory moments of discovery all the way to the end, our lives are filled with wondrous encounters and opportunities to create, even if we don't always have time to see them that way. As humans, we're in denial that we are animals, and that's thanks to our creativity. It shapes the way we see the world, allowing us to dream beyond our immediate, objective environments. We can allow ourselves to colour outside the lines, cut across the dotted lines, smudge the paint all over the canvas, and make up stories.

Creativity is uniquely human. But so is overthinking. And we excel at both. Our creative minds are great at taking us away from the present moment, far ahead into the land of expectations that we have of ourselves, others, and situations.

This is true of all creatives, and for professional creatives, it's where the balancing act can be at its most precarious. When creativity is your life and your livelihood, having undefined or unrealistic expectations means you risk ending up in the same blindfolded dash that I and so many of the people speeding aimlessly up the outside lane of our hypothetical highway ended up in.

Creative energy can resemble an AA battery: it has a positive and a negative side. When the battery is fully charged and properly connected, the positive and negative points create a circuit through which energy flows. The positive keeps us optimistic and moving forwards; the negative keeps us checking our speed and in touch with reality. But connecting the points up wrong breaks this healthy flow and produces a negative outcome. When a creative mind is incorrectly connected, it can begin to focus on the negative side and start to imagine negative outcomes, to catastrophise. Worse, it can begin to believe the catastrophic predictions it churns out. This can result in fight, flight, or freeze outcomes that have the potential to burn out the very creativity that created them — you could end up working obscene hours because you're too frightened to take a breather, give up because you can't meet undefined/unrealistic expectations, or become so lost and overwhelmed that you bury your head in the sand and do nothing.

Defining realistic expectations, whether related to income, workload, or clients, is vital when we're constantly being by bombarded by messages exhorting us to do more, do better, be better, stay better, know more, make more, get more, have more, 'hustle', 'grind'. The list is as long as it is meaningless. Know what 'enough' looks like for you and don't let the wind from those chasing the horizon blow you off course.

When the play becomes the income

It would be fair to say that many of us start out with romantic notions of where creativity might take us. "Choose a job you love, and you'll never have to work a day in your life" is a seductive, but unfortunately highly misleading cliché. We can find ourselves in the theme park of dreams, an eternal chance to play, to escape from the drab, soul-destroying, 9–5 world. We may have dreamed of becoming musicians, artists, authors, actors, or filmmakers.

Some of us still might. Some of us may still succeed one day. Some of us may even have already succeeded.

But even theme parks are businesses, and successful creatives are also businesspeople. And although that might make your inner idealistic teen roll their eyes in disgust, it's okay to make your livelihood from your self-expression, even if it's not in the field you dreamed it could be.

It's also worth remembering that the point of theme parks is to offer hyperreal experiences — and it's possible to lose sight of objective reality by becoming hooked on a self-generated version of the 'creative porn' described above.

To become a professional creative inherently entails a loss of innocence. This is as true for the Hollywood A-lister as it is for the illustrator working out of a cramped corner of their flat. The theme park of our dreams is a kind of Eden, and while making your creativity your living does mean you get to go on whichever rides you want, you also have to go beyond them, into the back offices. You have to deal with the advertising, the invoices, maybe even the hiring and firing — you have to sacrifice some of the innocence and purity that first attracted you.

Think of those moments when the ideas won't come, or too many come at once, or the phone doesn't ring, or it rings too much, or the client is too vague, or they micromanage you, or they expect you to reply to emails at 6 a.m., or 11 p.m., or they don't pay on time, and you soon reach the unpleasant realisation, remarked upon earlier, that this is not the easy ride you thought it would be. Taking religion away, the story of Adam and Eve in Eden still resonates as a parable of lost innocence. Once you're outside, there's no going back. Pandora's Box is open. And sure, if you're disgusted by the realities of making your play your work, you can always do something else, but while you can try to see everything with the same open curiosity as you did when you first started out — a concept known as 'Beginner's Mind' — you can never fully return to that pure state. In other words, you can't unsee what you've seen.

Ok, I am aware this all might sound a little too much, and there is a poignancy in realising that the world of professional creativity, as viewed from the outside, is a bit like a backdrop, behind which are a few props and a couple of overflowing bins. But we're here to embrace the positives, and stepping outside of Eden can equally be a liberating experience. To return to our car metaphor, would you rather be a kid who can't drive, staring awestruck at a gleaming high-performance sports car that you don't know how to use but dream of owning one day? Or would you rather be able to not only drive a decent car but also know how it works and how to get the best out of it?

The escape: a shortcut to instant gratification

Creativity comes from the soul — or if you don't believe in souls — from some kind of innermost desire. It retains that universal duality, that yin-and-yang, that AA-battery flow: it represents a need to express ourselves outwardly (even if only to ourselves), but it can equally be an escape from a mundane or even downright unpleasant reality. Even creatives whose work reflects, and perhaps even revels in, the grim crappiness of contemporary life tap into this flow. It can be a coping mechanism, helping us to define ourselves within or outside of a landscape we don't understand or even like. This isn't an inherently bad thing; the beauty and the power of being human is the ability to dream and create. Yes, birds can fly, but they can't imagine an entire world from nothing; they can't even change careers.

In the introduction to this book, when I was there, smoking my cigarette at 4 a.m., between 16-hour workdays, creativity — that wonderful human bounty — was my business, but it was also my escape route, my coping mechanism, and my way of finding acceptance and validation. All the time, as much as possible, and almost entirely unregulated. Growing up, did you ever play a game called Buckaroo? It involves a plastic mule on which you balance more and more items until it finally bucks and sends pieces flying everywhere. You can see where this is going: my creativity became the load-bearer for far too many things, and of course, it eventually bucked.

And so we return to the scales, to the balancing act. Humanity is creative, and creativity is human. There's precisely zero wrong with using creativity as a means of temporary escape and of gratification; if anything, it's healthy, and certainly healthier than wallowing in inertia or apathy. But when we start hanging too many things on it, when we define our entire worth through how creative we are or aren't being, then it becomes a drug as addictive and potentially destructive as any other form of instant gratification. We become like the friend that drinks to get blind drunk when the rest of the group can just enjoy a couple of beers — we need help. Just like those beers, creativity is a means of taking our minds away from the main issue or unsolved inner problems. At that point, it's time to slow down, be mindful rather than mind-full, and check in with what's going on.

Creativity in the 21st century -
what does it take to be (and stay) creative?

Creativity is part of the human condition, as old as our race and a vital part of how we became so dominant to begin with. But this is the 21st century we're talking about. The world is coming at our tribal hunter-gatherer brains faster and faster all the time. Stuff is blurring as it whizzes by. The ride is intense. We now absorb more information in one day than a mediaeval person absorbed in their entire life.[1] This upsurge feels relatively recent — I definitely feel like I'm expected to take in and retain more information per day than I was when I embarked on my creative career in the early 2000s.

What does this mean for us as creatives? Professionally or otherwise, do we have to accelerate our creative process(es) to keep up with how much faster humanity is operating? Do we even want to?

On one level, progress is not only inevitable but also incredible, and we adapt to it almost unconsciously. The blank page may be here to stay, but of the creative writers reading this book, I'd bet a decent amount of money that none of you use quills and parchment, or chalk and slate, or even typewriters. Sure, it's great to have an old-school notebook and a biro for sketching ideas, but writing a novel? Give me a laptop where I can get my ideas down

[1] Gaia Vince: 'Cities: How crowded life is changing us' (https://www.bbc.com/future/article/20130516-how-city-life-is-changing-us)

as fast as I can think of them. Go to a poetry night, and you'll see more and more performers reading from the notes section of their phone. Powerful home-studio software for musicians, pre-made templates and files for graphic designers. In that respect, one could argue, there has never been a better, more intuitive time to create.

Yet it's easy to get swept up in all the other stuff too. Unless we're hyper-niche, it's fair to say that most of us broadly keep pace with general fashions and trends, however subconsciously, because those are the clothes in the shops, the phones that technology has developed, the music that's current, the shows that are on TV, etc. It takes a special effort to become 100% out of step with your times.

This unintentional keeping up also extends to those metrics we discussed earlier — speed, size, and money. If we feel like everyone around us is being more creative more often, and possibly earning more money and accolades because of it, it's natural to want to stay in step. That's what's on offer, what's being presented to us as what everyone else is doing, right?

Most of the time, we hardly notice that we're keeping up. But increasingly, as the world continues to quicken and we're fed more and more information from every conceivable angle, it's like a treadmill gradually speeding up, and more and more of us are realising that it's getting too fast for us. Even those who seem to be keeping pace are likely a couple of notches away from being flung off backwards.

But we can adjust the speed of the treadmill if we want. We are the architects of our own busy-ness, and we always have the power to choose. Think of it as being like one of those Jimmy

Spice-style all-you-can-eat buffets that serve different kinds of food from all over the world. Want some spaghetti with a bit of tikka masala and some spring rolls? Fine. Want to make your play your work? It's hard work, but it is possible. Want to opt out and keep it to doodling for your own amusement? Perfectly valid. Want to do a bit of both? If you can comfortably balance it without bucking, then go for it!

And while we're mixing things up, I'm going to mix the metaphors and say this: don't let society hack the circuits to your theme park and send everything spinning out of control like some villain from a kid's cartoon. You are the architect, key-holder, and operator. It involves taking responsibility and ownership for your decisions, but it also brings you empowerment.

Meeting the untamed beast —
too many choices, lack of rules?

When we hone in on creativity, we find that, to a degree, progress shifts the ground beneath our feet. Yes, we do own the ability to choose and to define our expectations, but with the explosion in information comes more choice than ever before. We can do many more different kinds of creative work, we can be influenced by so many more different things, and we can share our creativity in many more different ways. There's Jimmy Spice's... and then there's a buffet with every conceivable food in the world.

I call this mass availability of choices the 'untamed beast'. The multiplication of options we have at our disposal makes final answers so much harder to calculate. What you do, how you do it, where you share it, how you share it. We can find ourselves wrestling with a Frankenstein-like monster that overwhelms our ability to harness our creative strengths.

Now, let's be clear: every human being has creative potential to a greater or lesser degree. Ask your kids if they've got any cool inventions, or ask your grandparents for the best route into town. They won't have any trouble coming up with multiple answers. Creativity isn't the issue; it's not a negative force; it's there to be cherished, nurtured, and celebrated.

But creativity is intertwined with our humanity, and just like our humanity, it ultimately has to engage with reality to have any chance of success, materially or spiritually. We might have to tussle with our optimism bias and inner romantic over this idea, but when the untamed beast is left to run wild, it hurts our creative outcomes. Ideas lose focus and projects never get finished, succumbing instead to eternal tweaking. Some might be happy to keep editing the novel they've spent 15 years writing — the escape is enough — but if we want to truly embrace our creativity and balance it with our humanity, then I would argue that we should adopt healthy habits and boundaries with our creativity as we would anything else in life that we want to enjoy the benefits of.

Creativity is an eternal lesson in growing resilience

Taming beasts and adopting positive habits takes a heap of willpower. If you don't already know from experience, creativity also requires building mental resilience, not least to the inevitable criticisms and rejections that come with any attempt at self-expression.

To wholly embrace your creative mindset can mean choosing to dedicate yourself to your practice with the discipline of an Olympic hopeful, the kind who trains almost daily for four years, aiming for that one shot at glory in an event that may only last seconds and be decided by an even smaller interval. They train to win, but they also learn how to process the struggle when the result goes the other way.

Creativity is your gold medal discipline, and ultimately, you know — or if you're unsure, you can work to discover — what it entails. You can practise it to your desired level, and through practise, you can build resilience. The knock-backs will always sting, and the issues mentioned so far will raise their heads time and again, but you can learn to deal with them and get back up more quickly every time.

If we nurture it, then just like our creativity, our resilience will continually evolve. So will our sense of balance as we get better at learning how much we can take and want to take, and as we learn to celebrate and be generous to ourselves and others on the same path, without giving too much of our power away.

This is perhaps the ultimate creative undertaking because it's one that we can never complete. Not because it's undefined or unrealistic, but because it involves working with the unfinishable project that is our humanity.

"In today's rush, we all think too much—seek too much—want too much—and forget about the joy of just being."

Eckhart Tolle

Pages

46 — 71

Chapter - no.2

Mind Full

Chapter - no.2

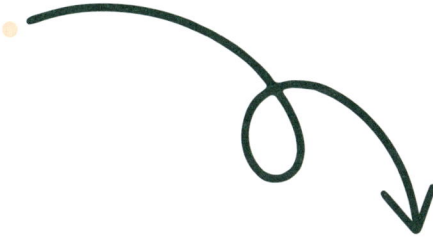

Where is your mind?

This section looks at how the creative and personal elements of our lives can conspire to overwhelm our minds.

The best place for us to start is to take a minute right now and ask yourself where your mind is at today. How are you doing? How much is on your mind at the moment? Are you looking out for yourself enough? If not, what action can you take, however small, to change that?

If/when you're in a position to probe a little further, take the time to consider some longer-term questions too: how much is too much for your mind? And, to return to something we talked about in the previous section, do you know where you're going? Few things can upset our mental scales more than a lack of direction, especially when we're travelling fast.

The honest truth

Here's the truth. You're most likely to consider buying and reading a book like this when you've gone past the point of those questions being able to help you avoid a crash — you're already in the ditch. We always think we can push it that little bit further ("after I finish this job", "once this invoice gets paid") before the shit hits the fan. This isn't a criticism; it's an observation, and whatever stage you've bought this book at, I congratulate you for having the intention to look after yourself from this point on.

Another honest truth is that no one has got it right all the time. However much they want you to believe otherwise (or however much you want to believe it), no one is happy, creative, or fulfilled all day every day. Everyone goes through ups and downs, both mental and material. No one's diary is perfect, and no one's portfolio is to their complete satisfaction. There's always some mundane worry or bother seeping through the cracks. You might think you'd love to have the kinds of worries that someone with a more glamorous portfolio or reputation has, but it's all relative.

Allowing yourself to realise this is both levelling and liberating. It dials up your compassion and empathy because you come to truly appreciate that beneath the sheen and the speed, behind the filters and the follower-counts, we creatives all have our fragile humanity in common. It's okay to admit that, the same as it's okay to ask for help. Just as importantly, if we are all essentially equal, then it follows that our creative peers only look better, smarter, stronger, and more talented if we place them on that pedestal, if we apply that filter.

This is obviously another balancing act, not an excuse for believing that no effort is needed because you're inherently as great as the most successful names in your field.

Even with luck and connections, it can take a long time, a lot of hard graft, and a few risks paying off to get a good thing going, especially if you're flying solo. It can also take a long time to understand and appreciate the power in the mirror. Realising that the people you thought so much better than you also suffer from doubts and worries won't automatically cure your doubts and worries.

Success, whatever that means to you, will forever be the sum of many parts in both your inner and outer worlds. New skills still have to be learned; crap jobs still have to be seen through; action and responsibility still have to be taken... You still have to show up. You still have to invest.

Investment

Like anything that requires cultivation or maintenance, your creativity and your creative business will reflect your investment in them.

If you don't polish your shelves, they'll get dusty; if you don't practise your skills, they'll get rusty.

Investing in your creativity obviously entails more than money. You also invest your time and your emotions. We're going to look at both here and explore where the sweet spot is and where too much or too little can create unnecessary pain.

Emotional investment

Our creative process and its output are hugely influenced by how much we care about it. At the start of our journey, we can make (or at least be prepared to make) an intense emotional investment in our work. After all, we are our creativity and vice versa. This is necessary because if we didn't start with high expectations of ourselves and what we could achieve, we'd never get anywhere.

From this hopeful starting point, two paths can generally be taken: you can keep investing your emotion in your work, striving for recognition, and building your reputation and portfolio. This is healthy so long as it doesn't become too intense and stray into obsessive perfectionism, people-pleasing, and/or outright megalomania — "I can and must do it all!"

The other path is perhaps more common, because it's downhill and therefore easier to take: we get used to achieving a certain standard of work and perhaps a certain safe level of income if we secure a couple of regular clients. We stop caring about whether we're credited for our work or not as long as it pays. We clock in, churn out, and clock off. As a result, tasks that once would have taxed our creative skills become like mechanical labour, and our creative powers can suffer as a result. We lose interest and become apathetic, which is particularly dangerous when you're running a business in a competitive field.

Emotional investment in what you do is important, especially in a vocation known for its high expectations. But as the warning on stock-investment websites goes, don't invest more than you can afford to lose. A half-arsed hack is no good to anybody, but neither is a burnt-out control freak.

If you're attempting to build a reputation in a field such as music, art, or literature, then emotional investment is absolutely vital. The majority who work for success in those fields have to begin without an audience or a network, and building both of those things can feel like trying to dig the foundations of a house, on your own, in the pouring rain. We struggle along without recognition, often without getting the lucky break or meeting the right person to champion our cause. But to have any chance of getting those things, we have to put something of ourselves into our work, and we have to put our work out there, which further eats into our actual creative time.

Creativity and time

Yet it's our creative time that must be cherished at all times. As our lives develop, and particularly when serious relationships and parenthood come along, we often have to work in the gaps, carving out small nooks of time here and there. But however long we get, it rarely feels like enough. It's a finite resource that holds infinite options. The more options we wish to explore, the more time we wish we had. The more we become involved in creative act, the more we explore and peel off the layers of possibilities, the more joy and satisfaction we get. It's possibly the only human activity immune to the law of diminishing returns — let me know if you ever come across someone who claims to have too much fun being creative and wishes they could do less. So many gratifying life activities stop being fun if we repeat them over and over. Eating, drinking, even sex could lose its potency if you did it three times a day every day. However, I'd happily bet my kids' inheritance that creativity, despite its multifaceted and turbulent nature, will always yield a return on your time and energy if explored with eternal intrigue and curiosity.

Every creative person longs for one thing and one thing only — the time and space to get lost in their craft. I've never met or spoken to anyone who has longed for less time creating and more time to focus on sending out invoices, chasing payments, and working out how to attract new clients (let alone little things like parenting, sleeping, eating, drinking, washing, doing the food shopping, keeping up with the laundry, etc.) Often, then, it's not a question of lacking the tools or options; it's more a lack of time, space, or even motivation.

Living in the world that's always on(line)

The world used to be more prescriptive about what career you could or should be expected to embark on — and stay in until retirement — but not anymore. Since the millennium and the progress we've made in its first two decades, anyone can pretty much do anything they like and forge a viable commercial career for themselves. The 'creative-career' tombola is filled with almost every conceivable creative journey if you're up for taking it.

However, this new found freedom to invent our careers comes with an even bigger supply of auxiliary activities that have become vital to our success. More than that, they're things we have to do to ensure the basic viability of our business. Creatives these days can rarely afford to be reclusive or enigmatic; social media has kicked down the door of our hideout and demanded to know what we're doing and how we're doing it. As well as artists, we may now feel pressured to be our own salesperson, manager, booking agent, accountant, PR executive, social media manager, photographer, videographer, and the rest.

But like most of the conundrums we've discussed so far, this situation can frighten or free you. And once again, it's always okay to ask for help. Sure, there are still people who try to jealously gate-keep knowledge, but there are also plenty of kind souls out there willing to share their experiences of establishing and maintaining a creative career. Furthermore, there are plenty of creatives out there, just like you, who are available to help you 'buy back your time', taking care of what, to you, are peripheral tasks and helping you free your schedule... and your mind.

There are certain pros and definite cons to a world that is always on(line), and the creative process benefits and suffers from them both, to the degree that we allow it.

For a start, we have never been exposed to so much inspiration before. If the internet (and social media in particular) has kicked down the door, it has also opened the windows and let the sunlight in. With a healthy mindset — one that doesn't see everyone else in your field as a potential threat and/or far better than you'll ever be — you can find endless inspiration from all over the world. Art, films, or music that might have taken years to find and cost hundreds to procure is likely now available to consume for free (or at least for a subscription). We gain access.

The process is demystified.

Likewise, we may no longer know our next-door neighbours, but we can now find our peers and potential networking opportunities without leaving the comfort of our sofa. We have the potential to engage and build an audience far more easily than we would have done 25 years ago, too. And crowded though it is, the internet is also theoretically unbounded — there is always space for you to carve your niche and build your presence.

Yet, as we know all too well by now, the online world has its downsides — downsides that are becoming ever more apparent as it becomes an inescapable part of daily life. Some of these we've already looked at — deceptive appearances, the compulsion to compare, and the desperate desire for an undefined 'more' (more followers, more likes, more click-throughs) — but there are others that can also affect our creative confidence. The light that comes in through the windows can soon become blinding.

For a start, we may feel the need to 'keep up' by constantly posting content, all of which takes time and effort to create and upload, especially if it's something like a reel to be posted across multiple platforms — to say nothing of the time lost to aimless scrolling, getting distracted by 'suggested posts', or the sudden urge to check what so-and-so is up to in their Instagram stories. Social media can play on our potential to develop FOMO (Fear of Missing Out) to a worrying degree.

Of course, any creative endeavour shared online will attract opinions, from the valid to the vile. No one likes a stranger with a bunch of numbers after their name and a clipart profile picture telling them that their work is worthless, but it's part of resilience training to either not read the comments, or at least not become emotionally entangled in them. Don't feed the trolls! Don't make the idiots happy.

Easy access and demystification have also led to the loss of romance and, obviously, mystery around the creative process. This can lead to issues, both in and of itself, and because you can so easily catapult to the other extreme — overexposure. People either get tired of seeing you posting all the time (or algorithms presenting your posts), or they become desensitised to your message. They scroll past, or even worse, click 'unfollow'.

Facing creativity in isolation vs. in a team

Creativity feeds on its surroundings, and so the creative environment can have a big impact on the creative process. I'm not (necessarily) talking about feng shui, but I am talking about whether you're creating alone or collaboratively. They're different approaches to the same thing, and they come with their own shortcuts and potential roadblocks.

Some creatives like to work alone. They need that space, that freedom, that quiet, maybe even that level of control. Trying to generate and refine ideas in a room full of other people can be distracting and unnerving. It can also be difficult to get your voice heard, and diplomacy can be the first thing to be thrown out of the window.

But with creative solitude comes the potential of creative loneliness. You might lack a network to bounce ideas off or get feedback from. Depending on the project you're working on, it may take longer, especially if you're committed to completing the auxiliary tasks around it yourself. There's no one else around to help talk you through a creative block, and unhelpful thoughts can quickly multiply when you're alone — especially when you stray onto social media: "I'm no good at this! Everyone else is better than me!"

The inverse is true of working in a creative team. There is the chance to get that vital spark from rubbing the bare twigs of ideas together, the chance to make something greater than the sum of its parts. There is the opportunity to learn from each other and to develop our skills. There's also perhaps the greater chance of structure and a shared workload. But if egos sneak into the room, then there can be little space for other ideas to be heard.

Getting out of our own way

Whether we're creating alone or in a silent room with a dozen other people yelling, one of the biggest things that can derail our creative train of thought is ourselves. We do it so often, so naturally, and in so many ways that being able not to do it can seem as much of a superpower as being able to create in the first place. We generally step on our own creative toes when we're either not clear enough about our self-imposed boundaries or when we overzealously apply them. We might, for example:

— Let our strong work ethic spill over into workaholism.
— Overthink everything and end up getting nothing done.
— Set or accept unrealistic deadlines and then rush work to meet them.

— Plan things too vaguely or not at all, and then either miss deadlines or have to rush work to meet them.
— Let perfectionism make us too hard on ourselves, hold us over-accountable, and judge ourselves by unrealistic standards (the kind we would never dream of judging others by).
— Succumb to some good, old-fashioned procrastination.

When this happens, our superpowers can become liabilities and drag us off the precarious tightrope one way or the other — and whether we fall into inaction or over-action, we fall out of the present moment and lose focus on what matters most: using our creativity to its best potential

The eternal impostor?

One of the most frustrating ways we can often throw a spanner in our own works is the dreaded 'impostor syndrome'. We might be totally confident in situations where many are unsure, but we might struggle to cope with situations that most people wouldn't bat an eyelid at — and this can mess us up, especially when we think we're being judged by others for it. We become terrified of being 'found out' somehow. We feel like we don't belong.

Impostor syndrome is by no means confined to the creative industries, or even the world of work. It can come as much from a social situation as being placed in a role or asked to do something that we feel is bigger than our skillset or knowledge. It can be all-consuming, and it can appear out of nowhere.

But what is an impostor? It's someone who's pretending to be something that they're not. To a degree, everyone feels like this at some point; it's an inevitable part of life, especially when we're trying to 'fake it 'til we make it'.

It's important to remember here that there's a world of difference between genuinely being an impostor (let's take identity theft as an extreme example) and impostor syndrome — worrying that, in our case, you're not a (good enough) creative. The latter has to do with self-doubt, the Achilles' heel of untold numbers of creatives throughout history, and it can be challenged and gotten through. If you're in a good position and have a strong reputation, you've likely worked hard for it; it won't have magically appeared. You deserve to enjoy it, and you will benefit more from enjoying it than if you will by letting those darker voices eat away at you and draw you away from the moment. Remember to remind yourself that you are doing ok, you are enough and you definitely belong where you are

When the work meets the feedback

In the first section, we looked at how creativity, when undertaken professionally, must meet reality at some point. This showdown generally happens when your client or your audience sees your work. This is one of the toughest tests of anyone's creative mettle — the moment when the email is sent, the files are uploaded, or the work is presented.

No one likes getting negative feedback, even if it's for work that, frankly, we've done on autopilot. But getting it when we feel we've done everything and more to deliver can cut deep. Even constructive feedback, however invaluable it is to our growth as creatives, can get to us, and embracing it is a skill that often has to be developed at odds with our ego; we have to manage our urge to get angry and fight back, to fire off a sarcastic email, or to withdraw and beat ourselves up out of all proportion.

As much as we can become emotionally invested in our work, these are the times when it's important to detach a little. We need an element of conflict in creativity, whether we like it or not. The conflict is essential to progress and growth

When the shit goes down

Of course, when external human factors are sapping our resilience — we might be having a bad day; we might simply be tired or hungry — our most laudable intentions go out of the window and we do take negative feedback to heart. It can chip away at our confidence — and chips and cracks are harder to fix than they are to make.

Sometimes, the damage is done way before the feedback: files will be corrupted, programs will crash, work will be lost. Other times, it will come after: clients won't pay on time, leaving you chasing up debts. Sometimes, it will just be one of those shitty jobs where nothing goes right.

And on top of the narrative arc of each project, you have the natural arc of your business to contend with: work might ebb and flow. However much you have a long-term plan, you still may find yourself overrun with work requests one month and then spend the following two months desperately wondering if you'll ever get a client again. This obviously affects income, and the one thing that drives so many people away from this lifestyle is a lack of financial security. In the beginning at least, you may have no guaranteed income, no holiday pay, and no company pension plan. It's a lot for anyone to take on before you even think about half of the stuff we've talked about.

But if you've come this far, you've clearly achieved a level of resilience that you can work from. You're not a video-game character who gets three chances and then has to start again; each time you hit an obstacle, you're still a little further through the game. You have that little bit more experience and resilience to draw on to get you through. And remember, no one has it together all the time. Even the most talented in your field go through down periods where they think they should jack it all in and go get a 'normal' job.

Ambitious anxiety

You know what you want. You believe that you can do it. You can achieve it. You just need the creative time to become it. But right at this second, you're feeling anxious because you don't seem to be making any progress. Or you're frustrated that you're not as far along as you want. It's the ultimate game of chicken-and-egg, and it only contains one player: you.

This is ambitious anxiety. It's another form of overwhelm, and it comes from believing that we're not yet what others might be right now. We're searching for our next hit, but it's still in the long grass, out of sight. We know it's there, but we don't know when it will show itself.

The problem here is that we convince ourselves that time isn't on our side. We feel like we're in a race where people are gliding past us with ease, snatching the finite amount of success there is, but we can't make ourselves go any faster. We can't create the work any quicker or any better.

Of course, ambition is no bad thing, but it's a cocktail that requires a healthy shot of reality and focus, otherwise it can motivate you to act impulsively, maybe even desperately without a considered plan of action. The results are often rushed and counter-productive: flawed products, launches that no one attends, podcast episodes that no one ever listens to, or YouTube channels that only your mum watches. In other words, we risk the one thing arguably more hurtful than negative feedback: total indifference.

We can only be where we are now, and we can only work with the tools that we have. We can (and should) always look to push our boundaries, but there are limits at any given time, and when we try and overleap ourselves, we often land flat on our face.

The goals you are trying to reach will likely always be there. Others may well reach them ahead of you, but that won't necessarily remove the goal from existence. There will always be more money to make and more briefs to win. People won't suddenly stop consuming the kind of thing you offer, whatever it is. Slow down and make a plan of how to get there.

Artificial Intelligence (AI)

We've spoken so far about the eternal and infinite nature of human creativity. We've also realised that we have to frame it within our 21st century existence. That being the case, we have to talk about AI.

Throughout history, humans have mechanised processes that have required us to use our bodies and minds, be it machinery, modes of transport, or calculators. Creativity itself has remained one of the few relatively unexplored frontiers, but now AI companies have built their drills on our land and are extracting information at a rate that would shame the most enthusiastic oil barons.

As a result, the face of creativity in the 2020s is morphing into an ominous ideas generator that can churn out in seconds what it might take a human days, months, or even years to achieve. It cannot do it very well yet (AI-generated content is easy to spot, and books written entirely by it are unreadably bad, generated imagery tends to look all the same and somewhat gloomy), but that's a moot point because it is learning at a frantic pace.

For some creatives, this is terrifying. There are plenty of disgruntled noises about AI-generated art and music, but there's also a sense of resignation. We've learned enough to realise that the tyranny of convenience is an invincible enemy — the mass of people generally don't care if something is made by humans or machines as long as it's there and easy to access.

For other creatives, AI is a tameable beast, one that can be house-trained to help aid creativity by offering prompts and insights. In this sense, something like ChatGPT becomes more like a calculator, Word, or Photoshop than some nameless evil stalking the land and laying waste to all in its path.

As the creative process holds infinite potential and generally infinite rewards, creative progress will continue to present new means, and these will inevitably become accepted ways of achieving our creative ends.

The inner critic

When you order a takeaway, eat a packet sandwich, or even shove something in the microwave, you barely need to think about the process of making the food, as you're barely involved beyond setting the right time and maybe giving something a little stir. If you begin cooking or baking things from scratch, then you become more invested in the process, but you're still likely following recipes worked out by others. If you get a little deeper into it, however, you might start deviating from the established ingredients; you might even start making your own recipes up.

Creativity is a little like this, especially when you dedicate yourself to it. You gain the confidence and the abilities to think for yourself, but you also take on board the increased chances of making a mistake (in some ways, we're back to our highway metaphor from the first section) — and it's these times when your inner critic can start turning up unwanted, making you question your decisions. And when you do make a mistake, it can begin to run around triumphantly, shouting, "Told you so!"

One of the major motivations of anyone who gets a creative

business together is the lack of a manager standing over our shoulder. But, if we allow it, our inner critic can quickly become the worst boss we've ever had. It can nag and berate us incessantly; from the moment we wake up to the time we lie there struggling to sleep. Heck, it can even wake us up in the middle of the night.

Without any kind of inner critic, you could argue that we might never hold ourselves accountable; we wouldn't bother to push ourselves in pursuit of our best work. But if outer criticism can be constructive or destructive, so can internal criticism.

The passer-by critic

Our creativity is often used for all kinds of ends. If you're the kind of person who creates for their own gratification, not to share or produce work, then quietening your inner critic is perhaps the end of your struggle. Those of us who are compelled to share our creativity, for whatever reason, inevitably encounter the passer-by critic.

Feedback from others can be fuel for our creative tank. It gives us reason to continue, even when completing a piece of work has felt like moving a mountain. Once that work is out there, getting positive feedback and encouragement on it can motivate us to see what we can achieve next.

However, encounters with strangers can sometimes bring us unwanted energy and feedback. It can be like putting diesel in a petrol engine, stopping us in our tracks. Worse still, it can drop a lit match into our fuel tank, igniting our inner critic and engulfing us in negativity.

Negative feedback, however warranted, unwarranted, justified, or unjustified, is something that our confidence is never quite ready for, however much we try and prepare ourselves for it. You can always remember that negative feedback tells you more about the person's state of mind rather than how good your work actually is

Mind full

The desire to create stuff, achieve goals, and conquer both internal and external criticism — and to be seen to do all of those things — can swamp our basic ability to function, let alone our creative engine.

The important thing to remember here is that 'busy' doesn't automatically mean 'good'. The 'busy fool' — someone who is always rushing around without actually getting anything done — is a very real person, and it's very easy to become one if we buy into too many of the myths described above and confuse appearances with reality.

Have you ever looked at a creative brief and felt like you couldn't cope? There's too much information trying to rush in all at once — and perhaps too many ideas trying to rush out at the same moment. I'm guessing that's not a state of mind in which you can rationally sit down and do your best work?

To have a full mind is to be overwhelmed, to have our engine flooded, bringing us to a forcible standstill sooner or later. Impostor syndrome might kick in; we might freeze and find hours have passed and we have nothing to show for it. Yet we might still feel stuck in a high gear. It can feel like pedalling furiously on a bike when the chain has come off.

We can only move when we have room to move in. This applies as much mentally as it does physically. If we jam our heads with things like impostor syndrome, negative self-talk, and unrealistic expectations on top of things like deadlines and ideas, then we don't so much get in our own way as box ourselves into a corner.

Here, the only way to move forwards is to stop fighting and surrender to the stoppage. Only when the wheels have stopped spinning quite so fast can you begin to catch your breath and say, "Right. Okay. What's going on here?" From that point on, some of the helping methods we've discussed in this book will make themselves apparent, and through purposeful slowing down, you can begin to find momentum.

"Information overload is a symptom of our desire to not focus on what's important. It is a choice."

Brian Solis

Pages

72 — 89

Chapter - no.3

Pause

Chapter - no.3

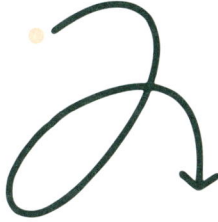

Change is needed

You've probably heard Einstein's famous quote: "The definition of insanity is doing the same thing over and over and expecting different results". This, of course, applies to methods that aren't working, but it can equally apply to us creatives when we get stuck in an unhealthy routine and keep going and going without taking care of ourselves. It's pretty insane to keep running around the same hamster wheel thinking that it will change anything. The only thing it will affect is our energy levels and ability to cope, and always for the worse.

Contrary to what you may have been told, sold, or come to believe, there's no wisdom in always working, always striving to be somewhere that you're not; it's a myth — we're back to the idea of the busy fool. In the creativity business, there are rarely prizes for hard work in and of itself; there has to be an output.

When we're going and doing all the time, however, it can be hard to read the signs — they go whizzing by or our minds are constantly preoccupied with something else. In most, if not all cases, the only way to make a difference is to slow... down... and... stop.

If you're stuck in gear and feel you have to keep moving (for fear of being left behind, for fear of missing out, for fear of acknowledging things that become harder to block out when you pause), then stopping to make a difference can seem crazily counter-intuitive. How are you going to get anywhere by stopping and standing still?

But we've also acknowledged that if you're reading this, then it's likely that something isn't working out for you, or you're at least concerned that something feels a little off. The only way to work it out, truly, is to stop. It's time for a change of action

How present are you?

Here's a true story about a pizza: after a long, whirlwind day of work and admin, I was balancing it all out by lying on an exercise mat and taking in guided deep breaths, as directed by my Pilates instructor. As ever, it was proving almost impossible to rid myself of my thinking overload, mulling over the dozens of things that had happened that day and were scheduled to happen the next.

As a result, I often spent the majority of this hour-long session trying to switch my focus and failing — and pulling some pretty unconvincing Pilates moves along the way. My thoughts just kept wandering backwards or forwards.

During one session, a rather stern and commanding instructor kept pacing the room, checking on everyone's progress.

During one particularly deep stretch, which we were meant to be focusing on with our breath and our mind, she asked me what I was thinking, presumably hoping that all the stretching we'd done to reach this climactic point was worth it.

"Fiorentina," I replied, giving my honest thoughts at that moment. "Definitely having a Fiorentina pizza after this." She looked confused and asked if I was trying to be funny. I didn't have time to be funny; I was busy thinking about my dinner. "Of course I'm not," I replied to her with her visible dismay about the whole exchange.

This incident sums up the daily battle I had, not only with all the aspects of my work but also with myself. To counter the overwhelm I felt from overloading myself, I tried to incorporate helpful around-the-work activities, such as Pilates, into my day. But all it ultimately meant was another battle: if the short walk to the studio wasn't enough to disengage, I therefore felt I had to work doubly hard so that I could finish earlier and give myself a little more time to unplug and therefore feel the benefit of the exercise. Just reading that sentence is exhausting to me now, let alone living it

Audit yourself

What do you see when you look in the mirror? Assuming you're present enough to assess what you see, are you looking at you, as you actually are? Are you seeing who you want to be? What you lack? Are you seeing someone whose identity is so enmeshed with their work and their creativity that those things are no longer separable? As creatives, we can feel ourselves deeply connected to our work, and of course, our most authentic work always has something of us inside it, but just like it's important to stop, it's also important every so often to untangle ourselves and our process from our output and look objectively at both — the chicken definitely comes before the egg here. Are you defining insanity by doing the same unhelpful things over and over again?

The first thing to audit is your lifestyle. That way, you can gain an understanding of the mindset that you approach your creativity with. From the way this chapter started, you might be forgiven for thinking that a 'busy' lifestyle only applies to those who are in a similar situation to my former one: always working on briefs, phone ringing off the hook, new emails every five seconds, as little sleep as possible to keep the wheels turning, etc. But if we remember the anxious anxiety of the previous chapter, we realise that we can find ourselves stuck in unhelpful busy patterns at any other stage.

For example:

— You might be struggling to find work and clients — definitely at the ebb end of the ebb-and-flow of professional creativity — and either be doing nothing but worry, or still moving at the same rate as when you're busy, still going through the same old motions (content mills, sites where you pitch and bid for work as cheaply as possible, "do an unpaid sample for us", etc.) that are keeping the wheels spinning but getting you nowhere.

— You might be anywhere between dead and overrun as far as work is concerned and be equally consumed by ambitious anxiety — you're still not where you want to be (or feel you should be); others have more high-profile/ better paid/interesting work than you. This might lead you to make poorly thought decisions that waste your time and your money, particularly if you're desperate to find work.

It should hopefully be clear from looking at all of these very different situations that they're all screaming out for the same answer: STOP!

It's vital that we, as creatives, make the time, preferably before we crash, to step away from our lifestyle, stop hammering away at the coalface, and create some space between us and it. The view is so much clearer when we can get up high, above the imposing buildings and smog of our everyday tasks and worries, see it as a whole, and appraise our lifestyle. Then, you can see what is working for you, and what is defining insanity, and begin planning to make changes accordingly.

So far, so inspiring, but also vague. What does auditing yourself actually look like? It's really pretty simple — as long as you're honest with yourself.

— The first practical step you can take in a lifestyle audit is to keep a record of your days. Note down what you do and how long it takes you (all of it, including time spent getting distracted by social media, looking at the news, playing games on your phone, giving time to tasks that slow you down or add to your workload, etc.)

— Keep a food diary. This isn't implying that you need to diet, but sometimes we can eat less healthily than we think simply because we don't notice or we think we'll compensate for the takeaway/complete lack of food the next day (without realising that we do the same thing three days in a row). If you feel like crap after eating food, the answer is often in the takeaway box. And what we put into our bodies can really impact what happens in our minds.

— Over the course of a week or so, note down how much time you spend socialising, how often you go out (as in spend time outdoors), what exercise you get, how much time you spent on your mental development (reading, learning, etc.) Did your cognitive overload and long hours of work make you feel socially awkward and anxious?

— Keep a mood diary. Note down how you feel throughout the week. This will help you get an overall picture of where your mind is at. Negative thoughts tend to cloud our judgement and often override the happier moments.

— Ask your friends and family how they think you're doing right now. An outsider view can provide you with a valuable perspective.

After seven days of this, you can get a realistic idea of where you are right now. You can even structure it into sections or columns covering work, general life admin, play, and rest, giving you a clear visual idea of how your life is divided up. Finally, calculate how your time is spent in percentages — for example, Work = 75%, Life = 15%, Rest = 10% — and you will quickly see how your scales require rebalancing.

If you find you're spending an unhealthy amount of time on work (or equally, an unhealthy amount of time doing everything to avoid work), then this is an ideal time to observe your thought processes as well — you may have already noticed them as you've kept a record of your day. Are there any strong or negative habits? Is there resistance to change? Or resistance to stopping or to doing? Do you head for social media as a way of avoiding dealing with these thoughts?

Schoolteachers are fond of saying, "If you cheat in an exam, the only person you're cheating is yourself." And the same principle applies here. There are no prizes or plaudits for having (or pretending to have) a healthy, balanced lifestyle and mindset. The only people who gain or lose are you and those around you. Remain honest with yourself about why you're doing what you're doing. What's driving your mentality that way? Is it fear of stopping? Ambitious anxiety? Overwhelm? If you genuinely don't know, then it really is time to stop and ask

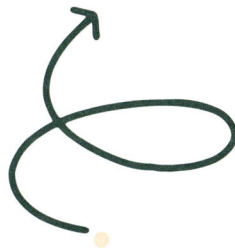

Auditing your work

Once you've audited the person who does the work, then you can hone your attention on the work being done. This is a time for you to take a step back from the bit of the canvas you've been working on and appreciate how it fits into the whole painting. You might take your entire portfolio, or if that's too big a task, you might review the last 12 months, or the last 6, whatever makes sense to you and whatever helps you best appreciate your progress to this point.

There are some basic key questions you can ask yourself, honestly and dispassionately (i.e., they're not an excuse to berate yourself or unfairly compare your work to others):

— How has your work evolved over the time-frame you're looking at? Has it improved? Or have you been doing it on autopilot recently?

— Do you remember most of the work, or is it all a bit of a blur of new clients and commissions?

— How much of your recent work did you actually enjoy producing? Did you make the right call in accepting work that helps you grow, or are your choices giving you more work that doesn't align with your hopes and long-term aspirations?

— Outcomes aside, what have you learned by doing this

work? Have you deepened your understanding of what you're doing? For example, if you're a graphic designer, have you developed new skills? Do you put together designs that are a little subtler or more complex? If you're a writer, have you widened your vocabulary or improved your grasp of grammar, or have you become a cliché generator?

— Are there any constants in your work? Do the same themes, ideas, words, or images keep cropping up? What is that telling you?

— What are the wins in your work? Are there any pieces, or even pieces of pieces, where you think, "Yep. Nailed it there"? Did you take time to celebrate the good stuff, or just move straight to the next project?

— What have been the learning curves? Have there been any mistakes or outright fuck-ups? And if so — equally as important — have you learned from them?

— You can also ask other, trusted and honest people in your network for their opinion. How do they see your work and/or business as an observer?

This kind of honest audit can work surprising wonders for your confidence, especially if you can remain open to it. If you were as atrocious as your untamed inner critic or impostor wanted you to believe, you wouldn't be in a position where you had a portfolio to review; you simply wouldn't have had any work.

To some, such a process might feel a bit like an annual review with the boss, the kind of daft corporate dance that we went into business to try and avoid. But it does have creative value and helps you re-orientate yourself. You're always going to be further along on your journey than the last time you stopped and looked around, and it can be inspiring to see how far you've come — far more inspiring than scrolling through other people's portfolios and worrying that yours doesn't look quite like theirs.

Many of you reading this or embarking on this kind of life-and-work audit will be doing so from the position of having crashed. And whether you stumbled or hurtled off course:

— There will have been warning signs that were missed.

— It likely won't be the first time.

That's okay. You're reading the words of someone who kept going and going, running red lights, and smashing through barriers.

The important thing to do is to recognise it so that you can better spot the signs and take useful corrective action.

Take the time to sit and reflect on your career, maybe even your life up to this point. When have been the times that you've burnt yourself out or driven yourself over the edge? What caused it, and can you remember how long the build-up was each time? Have you had a series of burnouts that have increased in intensity over time? Importantly, are there any things that you keep doing or forgetting to do that are causing them?

Honest self-knowledge, untainted by our neuroses or the (perceived) judgements of others can be one of the most powerful tools we will ever use — as long as we use it and action what it tells us. That might sound obvious to the point of corniness, but we misuse or fail to use our power all the time. Think of the gym memberships we take out and never use fully or at all, how we use something as powerful as the internet to watch TikToks and squabble in comments sections, the times we stay out doing vodka shots or binge a TV series knowing full well that we'll likely be too hungover or tired to function properly the next day

Unplug

And so, having looked in the mirror, looked back, assessed, and appraised, there comes another, perhaps even more daunting challenge: unplugging.

The more we live, work, and generally can't do without the world that's always on(line), the frankly scarier the idea of leaving it, even if just for a day, becomes. Your mind can doubtless generate multiple excuses for why you, of all people, need to stay plugged in at all times. It's your work; it's your business; it's your life. Phone on the bedside table whilst you sleep, in the kitchen while you're cooking, in your lap whilst you're watching TV, in the bathroom while you shower. Notifications on at all times, and scrolling even if there aren't any. When you wake up, at mealtimes, before you go to sleep, when you wake up in the night, whilst queueing, on the toilet, on holiday, on the bus, on the train, in the passenger seat. And let's be honest, we all know from *that* furtive downward glance whether someone's on their phone whilst driving.

Unplugging is good for you, and that doesn't only apply to social media; avoiding watching TV news and reading newspapers can help too. Having audited your life and work, one of the positive changes you can make, if you don't already do it, is to schedule in a set time to unplug (perhaps an evening or a day of the weekend). Find time for yourself. Yes, social media does hold all kinds of potential for our creativity and our business, but our creative minds simply cannot take the constant overload, and our creative potential and creative time are wasted by endless and aimless scrolling through, let's face it, vapid, repetitive crap that leaves your mind as soon as it leaves your screen (if it ever goes in at all).

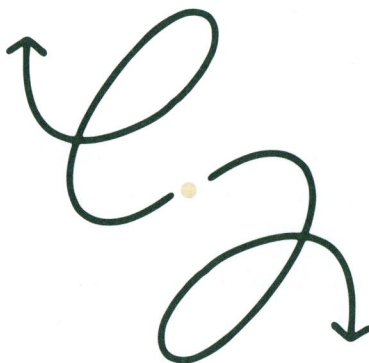

"The real man smiles in trouble, gathers strength from distress, and grows brave by reflection."

Thomas Paine

Pages

90 — 109

Chapter - no.4

Define

Chapter - no.4

Define 'you'

In the last section, we took a look back over our shoulder at our journey to date and made an honest audit of how we'd gotten to the stage we were at, and in particular, any bad habits that had helped to derail us along the way.

As valuable as this process is, it's important to remember throughout that you are not your mistakes, and so having defined where you are, the next step is to define who you are. You might think it should be the other way round — surely the self comes first — but I'm pretty certain that you don't feel that you're the same person you were when you started your creative journey. In that sense at least, your journey so far greatly informs who you are now. And as the present moment is essentially all any of us have, that's the best place to define yourself in.

In other words... Who are you? Right now. Who are you?

The further you get from your immediate details — name, address, DOB, relationship status, whether you're a parent or not, job description, political and religious beliefs, etc., the broader the definitions you can find yourself wrestling with. This seemingly simple, three-word question can quickly become an untamed beast in its own right.

However, armed with the knowledge that you are a creative and that you want to define yourself in that context — and having audited your journey to date — you can begin to make some relevant definitions about the kind of person you know yourself to be here and now. The temptation might be to load these definitions with judgements, but look to keep your beginner's mind and merely observe.

Still no clearer? Then look at it this way: without thinking of your answer as 'good' or 'bad', do you tend to be:

— A fighter, flighter, or a freezer?
— A sprinter or a marathon runner?
— Cautious or all-in?
— Experimenter or traditionalist?
— Leader or follower? Introvert or extrovert?
— Little-and-often or everything-at-once?
— Are you a happy procrastinator or an early finisher?
— Low-key or out-there?
— Do you keep yourself to yourself or strive to influence?

The list goes on: do you think best when you're still or moving, or mixing the two? How do you cope with negative situations or confrontation? Are you empowered by people paying you positive attention, or does it feel like the whole world's singing

'Happy Birthday' to you and you don't know where to look? How comfortable are you asking for help? How do 'you' make choices in life because of who 'you' are? Do you embrace who you are, or do you wish to make amends for better outcomes? Which of these has been your Achilles heel and what has become your identity? It's a lot of questions, I know. But your answers to them will lead to clarity

Define your 'enough'

Life often comes at us with the force of a blizzard. When you're in the epicentre of your own storm, you can become blind to what's around you. We carry on with our story, day in, day out, and we often don't recognise the smallest of changes that happen gradually.

It's massively helpful to look back and pinpoint the times when you've gone through the biggest burnouts or even breakdowns of your life, as well as all the little tremors and rumblings that came beforehand. If you keep putting it off, you'll eventually reach a point where you'll have no choice but to deal with it — and you'll have to do so from a position of total burnout.

Burnout doesn't happen over the course of a single, isolated day, and it isn't caused by just one part of our life or work going rogue. The series of events and identifiers should be revealing to us what's happening on the outside and inside. Knowing what you do and don't want, what works and what doesn't, can be invaluable when you want to get your shit together — and keep it together.

When you hit burnout, you haven't had enough; you've had too much. So, by looking at your past burnouts, and what caused them, you can probably mark the point that represents your 'enough' in terms of enough work, enough rest, and enough play. It's easy to apply this only to busy-ness, but it can help to equally define it for the times when business is a little slower: at what point does your output arc from being constructive to counter-productive? What are the limits of your (super)powers?

There is also the obvious material 'enough' of money to define. This is one of the hardest enoughs to grapple with. Realistically, in the long term, none of us want to work just to cover the bills; we want disposable income at some point as well. But financial gain has to be weighed against all the other costs that achieving it takes. Be honest about your skills, your market, and what you can expect to earn, and decide on a figure that would, realistically, keep you happy without upsetting your work, rest, and play balance.

Define your inner obstacles

Our creative journey has often become complicated even before we start. We come to it with our past in tow. We all have a different load to carry, and however much we claim that we are starting afresh, wiping the slate clean, and becoming the best, most efficient versions of ourselves, we always do so in the shadow of what has gone before.

Our basic mindset is formed at a very young age. The first critical period of brain development in children occurs between the ages of two and seven (Greek philosopher Aristotle wrote,

Define

"Give me a child until he is seven, and I will show you the man.") This means that, realistically, we have little chance to influence the quantity and quality of what we're going to carry with us. As we mature, we can choose to take charge of our emotional baggage; we can choose which bits serve us and which don't. However — and again, this is an honest truth, not a loaded judgement — so many of us end up carrying that baggage without realising: we deny its existence or simply aren't in touch enough with ourselves to know it's there

Define your spark

Happiness is what happens when our expectations meet or are surpassed by reality. You're also more likely to feel happier as a result of action that didn't present itself as something extraordinary. Think of how Thursday evening, and the anticipation of Friday, can often be more exciting than Friday itself, or how spontaneous nights out are always more enjoyable than massive parties that are hyped up for weeks beforehand. That 5k run you did, even though you really didn't feel like it, often tends to provide a few personal PRs and a hit of endorphins to reward you for getting out there.

Although we may not realise it, happiness can put us into a strange bind too: we may not have our happiness threshold (realistically) defined, but at the same time, we can subconsciously make it our life's work to try and feel just that little bit happier. But when does the latter process stop? Does your life need to be on an upward curve all the time? Is exponential growth needed until the day you die? Or just until you retire (whichever comes first)?

When we're on the move, up and across our daily tasks and successes, we're so preoccupied with managing our work process and juggling many different expectations — both our own and those around us. It's therefore harder to pause and define our expectations for something simultaneously as vague and necessary as happiness. Surely, like creative time, you can't have enough of it, right?

The issue is that by not defining what happiness means to us, and specifically not defining it in the present moment, we keep it ahead of us in the distance, a perfect donkey-and-carrot scenario. The feeling that there's never enough work coming in, or if there is, that it's not quite the kind we want; that there's only projects that don't make our creative portfolio look good. Add social media into the mix and you end up potentially chasing little pieces of what look like happiness but are merely scraps of dopamine that constantly leave us wanting more. Do you know how many 'likes' you need to feel it's enough? Will that enough change over time if you don't get the numbers you want?

A humble person will presumably start with low expectations of what they might get back from putting themselves out there. Small impressions make corresponding ripples. But like your creative process, your creative business is a process. Small steps can beget giant steps, and so from humble beginnings, you can build your business and your expectations. In this sense, what makes us happy is always changing. It's worth checking in from time to time to update your definition of happiness. What actions bring about that calm, sure sense of happiness? It could be anything from simply being able to cover your outgoings to helping someone out to completing a challenging piece of work and feeling that you're growing both as a person and a creative

Define your focus

For many creatives, one of the most alluring aspects of starting a creative business is escaping the Monday – Friday, 9 – 5. If you work in it and don't enjoy it, then the idea of not having to do it, of having more control over your hours, can look like an oasis in a desert.

But the desert can also conjure mirages, and it's so easy to start dreaming that you're escaping the rat race altogether. But guess what? Yep, stuff still needs doing. The creative work, the admin, all the little side tasks. The likelihood is, particularly if you go it alone, that you'll have full-time work and then some.

If you do this without knowing and defining your focus, then all hell can break loose. You can end up becoming disorganised, forgetting to reply to emails, running out of time, making mistakes, and generally getting overwhelmed. When we lose focus, our mind wanders. We take our eye off both the goal and the ball and can end up feeling deeply stressed and unhappy. That way too lies burnout.

It can be hard to do at first, especially if you're brand new to your field, but you should fairly quickly be able to identify quite a few things about yourself and your routine:
— How much time you realistically have available to work in a day/week.

— What time of day your creative energy and problem-solving skills are at their strongest.

— When you're most likely to have the patience for admin.

— What your time-thieves are
(phone, TV, family, hangovers, etc.)

— When you benefit the most from unplugging
(before bed, on a weekend, etc.)

Defining all of this and giving yourself a margin of error is hugely important, too. Whether you put it there or not, there will always, always, be something in your way to distract you from your work. It doesn't matter how meticulous or absent your organisation skills are, life is a whack-a-mole machine that will keep things popping up from all angles — an email that needs a quick reply; your laptop, phone or printer deciding to simply stop working; an ill child or closed nursery, a bad night's sleep, a relative ringing for a chat, a cold-caller wanting to upsell you something, roadworks right outside your window, your dog eating your notepad - the chances that you will be able to sit down, uninterrupted, every day, and just do what you want to do and nothing more, are infinitesimally small.

With this in mind, when you define your focus and plan your time around it, don't straitjacket yourself into unrealistic time frames, because more often than not, something will happen to upset your schedule, and without that flexibility, everything can quickly become unfocused

Define your denial

We humans are very good at finding ways around obstacles. For creative humans, it's definitely one of our superpowers. We either deal directly with the thing that's in our path, or we find a creative way around it.

And denying the existence of a problem is a very good way of getting around it. At first.

We do this all the time. The (creative) human mind excels at reasoning why we need to drink that extra glass of wine, order that takeaway, skip yoga this week, have a day off, or pull an all-nighter to finish just this one bit of work. We can perform flawless mental gymnastics to convince ourselves that even though we've done the same thing for weeks on end, it's not a habit; we'll simply do better tomorrow when things are different.

But denying our way around obstacles doesn't work. It's like making the minimum payment on a credit card month after month. The same issue simply reappears further up the path, a little bigger every time, until eventually, it blocks our way and has to be dealt with, often far more painfully than if we'd sorted it out earlier. What's worse: getting a check-up at the dentist for a little niggle or waiting until you've got an abscess?

One of the most important parts of being honest with yourself is being honest about what you're not being honest with yourself about. It's easier to step over a pebble than it is a boulder.

Define your fears

It's fair to say that denial is essentially a form of fear: fear of facing up to facts about yourself. So while you're under the hood, having a look around and defining your denial, it's also worthwhile listing down things you're afraid of. Specifically, keep it to things that pertain to your creative process and business — unless a spider walks across your computer screen, your arachnophobia is unlikely to hinder the running of your business.

Are you:

— Afraid of failure (work not good enough, won't be able to pay the bills, won't get enough clients, etc.)

— Afraid of rejection (getting negative feedback, rejection letters, no replies, no interaction on your social media channels, etc.)

— Afraid of being vulnerable (putting yourself and your creative work out there, asking people for work and/or money, etc.)

— Afraid to stop (can't turn work down, can't take a day off, can't say "enough" because if you do, it will all come crashing down and you'll never get any work again.)

If you can tune in and recognise those fears in yourself, then acknowledging them can put you on the path to challenging them. Any fears you face over your creativity and your business have already been felt by untold numbers of creatives before you, and there are plenty of specific resources out there that can help you to solve/manage them, even if they've become overwhelming

Define your addictions

Certain memories are impossible to escape. They can't be wiped off the register just because we now have a different view of our past. When I was staying with my great-grandparents on the outskirts of my town as a small child, there wasn't much happening. Beyond the gigantic pear tree and rows of planted fruit and vegetables in their front garden, I guess the sole exciting feature was the barrel of fermenting plums that my great-granddad stored for his homemade brandy production. He wasn't exactly running a speakeasy, although it's much funnier to think of it like that now, and not something I appreciated at five years old. The stillness in time of that reality, living away from the town, is something I find nearly unthinkable in my current life in the world that's always on. Yet I have fond memories of it: I helped to bake cakes, chop wood, and move coal in the basement. It all feels like a black-and-white movie compared to the hyper, vivid, technicolour life I lead now. And that's kind of the problem. We have become scared of stillness in time. At least, I feel that way more often than not.

I still vividly remember the sound of the wind-up clock in their living room. The inescapable 'tik-tak' sound that pierced the silence every second. Every swing of the pendulum made itself the most important part of the room. Thinking about it, I bet this experience is shared by many of my generation. Having sat through hours of this experience could have easily made the first line of a horror script of how boredom could turn into a violent thought in the digital age. But I didn't know any better. Whilst I was busy eating pears from my great-gran's enormous tree, Steve Jobs was living a diet of apples and busily putting together his first fruit company product on the other side of the world.

Our pockets are hiding our windows to the most processed dopamine-on-steroids-mixed-with-cocaine parallel reality. One that we could never have imagined even 20 years ago.

There could be any number of reasons that we start reaching for our phone every minute — boredom, intrigue, novelty value — but it can quickly become a difficult habit to break, especially when it's all so easy: simply point a camera at yourself, press the red button and the ideas and thoughts that were mere seconds ago a private situation are now out in the open for the world to see.

Define your future self

For all of its benefits, a creative career can be a choppy one — it's certainly not for the faint of heart! It can challenge, frustrate, and overwhelm you. But it can simultaneously be the making of you, bringing out your very best attributes and pushing you to achieve things you never thought possible.

The best way to navigate it, therefore, is to take the time to reflect and honestly define yourself in all of the ways described in this section. By both looking back and taking account of where you are right now, you can best begin to plot a course towards the future. You can better define the kind of mindset you'll need and the best actions to take.

So, the final definition to make is what you want your future self to look like. This sounds like the dreaded "where do you see yourself in five years' time?" interview question, but it's so much more than that. Your definition of your future self, when built on the foundations of how you've defined parts of your past and present, can be the line that you hold on to when crosswinds try to blow you off-course. If you know where you're going and how you're going to get there, then it can be surprisingly easy to adapt when things don't go to plan.

Consider some of the following when working out the who, where, why, and how of your future self:

— **Who do you envy?** We use envy and jealousy interchangeably, but jealousy is based on fear, whereas envy can be energising and motivating. If we're jealous of someone, then we want to snatch what they've got and have it for ourselves. If we're envious, then we want to have what they have too, but without taking it from them. In this context, defining whose creative career you're healthily envious of can point the way forward.

— **What motivates you to self-start?** No one's going to hand you a creative career; you have to go out and build it for yourself. This means showing up and making it happen. You're only going to keep doing that through the inevitable tough times if you're genuinely motivated by what you're trying to achieve. So define what makes you want to show up even when you don't have to.

— **What risks are you prepared to take?** Are you a gambler, or do you prefer to stick with the tried and tested?

— **How open are you to collaboration?** Are you a one-man-band who has a very set vision of how things should be, or do you find working with others brings out the best in you?

Define your support

Finally, for this section, it's crucial to define your support network: the people who can offer practical advice, encouragement, and who'll also be there to listen and advise when things aren't going so well.

Just like raising a child, growing a creative career takes a village, even if you're a solo freelancer. No one, not even the most gifted of people, can manage every area of their personal and professional lives effectively without any kind of help or support.

It's also important to have the right kind of people you can turn to. For example, if you're struggling with a creative commission, then is turning to a friend or family member with no experience or interest in that area going to be the best port of call? If you're feeling overwhelmed by your work, then is a fellow professional in the same field who believes in 'shutting up and just getting on with it' going to give you the healthiest advice?

Sometimes, your network might benefit from being expanded to include professional help in the form of therapy. This is something that the next section looks at in more detail.

"Rowing harder
doesn't help
if the boat
is headed in
the wrong
direction."

Kenichi Ohmae

Pages

110 — 131

Chapter - no.5

Help

Chapter - no.5

123. Need the nudge?

124. *Taking action*

125. Accepting what you cannot change

126. *Therapy is a journey, not an operation*

127. Therapy for everything and everyone...

128. *...And that includes you*

Growing up "normal"

Welcome to a world where everyone is doing great and most of all 'normal'. I grew up in a world just like it. I know this because everyone assured me (and themselves) that they were nothing out of the ordinary, just regular members of society. No one's actions stood out, and no one ever complained or asked for help with anything, let alone their state of mind.

But whatever they said, and however rose-tinted the past can seem, people were seldom genuinely happy and life was rarely simple. The struggle to cope and to maintain a veneer of ordinariness left many craving some kind of vice to make it from one relentlessly 'normal' day to the next — booze, cigarettes, dope, abusing painkillers, and skating white rails being the easiest props.

If you admitted you were struggling and sought professional help, you ran the risk of being diagnosed as 'crazy' or 'mad'. There was little of the nuanced understanding that we have around mental health today; it was that cold and that black-and-white. You either kept your head down and muddled through, or you were ripe for locking up and analysis by clinical psychiatrists — with little hope of being let loose in society ever again.

It sounds like something from a dystopian thriller set in a terrifying future, but this was the atmosphere of my childhood and adolescence. And it's still a worryingly prevalent attitude across many societies today.

How we've changed our minds about our minds

The further back in time we look, the worse the stigmas around mental health seem to us. For centuries, many serious forms of mental issues and diseases were, by today's standards, treated appallingly. With some obvious exceptions, this was due to a lack of understanding rather than evil intent; but ill people would often find themselves not only banished to the fringes of society but also labelled contagious. Like the old laws that made suicide illegal, I don't think it really helped.

We know now that you can't 'catch' mental health problems in the same way you catch a cold, although there are studies looking at whether trauma can be genetically inherited. On top of the foundations laid by our upbringing, our environment clearly plays a part in how we feel and how we experience our surroundings.

Today, the pendulum has, or at least appears to have, swung to the other side. We're now far more aware, informed, and educated about mental health. It's far higher up our list of priorities. The emergence of mindfulness and our increased awareness of mental health in recent years have played a major part in this: apps such as Headspace and Calm, yoga on YouTube, 'hygge', and self-care titles. Even colouring books for adults have helped to bring the idea of non-toxic self-care away from new-age woo-woo and into the mainstream. 'Normal' people are now at least a little more likely to find moments of quiet and solitude and spend some time on themselves. But there is one word that is still strangely taboo

The T-word

Yes, that taboo T-word is... Therapy. And we're going to talk about it.

When I was a child, conditioned by the 'normal' attitudes of a mid-sized central European city, in-person therapy was something that only happened in Hollywood movies. For years afterwards, even long after I moved to the UK in my early twenties, it still seemed exotic and more than a little eccentric. Only more recently have I realised that even those who grew up at the wealthiest epicentres of western culture saw therapy as the preserve of the rich and famous. So, if therapy was a thing, how and where did it happen?

Growing up, no one I knew ever talked about therapy. If they had sessions (which I doubt), it would have been easier for them to come out as gay than admit they were working through difficult emotions — and that's saying something about their feelings. Things are a little different now, but such attitudes weren't confined to the time and place I was raised in — and they still aren't. It will take years, maybe even decades, for mental-health therapy to become an accepted part of everyday life.

Yet there's no reason why therapy should have been taboo in the first place, let alone for the stigma to linger. We go to the gym to help our bodies become healthier and stronger; we take our car to be serviced; we even test plug sockets every so often to make sure they won't electrocute us the next time we charge our phone. But services to help us look after our minds are either unaffordable to the majority or, where available on public health services, such as the NHS in the UK, have enormous waiting lists (which in itself is very telling). As a result, so many of us self-medicate and/or find small issues eventually ballooning into huge complexes that are more deeply entrenched and much harder to fix.

Now, I stress that I'm no expert on clinical therapy. Nor is this book in any way intended as therapy. If you're in a situation that is impacting your life and your health, then I urge you to seek professional help. What I want to do here is to share my experience and my journey through therapy, a journey that has now lasted for more than a decade and been far more unpredictable than I ever could have, erm, predicted.

Let's start at the end

Just over a year ago, I was standing in the paddock of a livery yard, holding a lead rope attached to a Shetland pony called Abel. A therapist was asking me questions. I was a few metres away from the other people looking after the yard, topping up water buckets, and mucking out stables, etc. Despite their presence and my usual reticence about public displays of emotion, tears were streaming down my face and there was no part of me holding them back. It was my first equine therapy session, and I didn't care where I was or what was happening to me. I was finally feeling my feelings and making peace with what happened in my past, helping me to become more at ease with my current-self and enabling me to move forward in my life.

It may have been my first equine therapy session, but it had taken 10 years of other therapies for me to reach this stage: a place where I felt a sense of long-term progress. There had been a lot of work, and there was still a long way to go.

Just like us, therapy comes in different shapes and sizes to fit our individual needs. It doesn't necessarily mean lying on a leather couch in a sterile office telling a Freud lookalike about your father; it can be in-person, online, with your partner, and even with horses. Furthermore, it doesn't necessarily have to probe your past; there are coaching-based therapies to help you with specific issues in the here-and-now, such as nutritional therapy.

There are therapeutic apps available; there are YouTube channels, TikToks, and podcasts. Many of these, including this book, might not be substitutes of therapy itself, but they can act as a gateway, leading you to find the best kind of therapy for you and the load that you're dealing with.

However, from my experience I strongly suggest engaging in in-person sessions, even just to get started and navigate the next step correctly. Amazing things can happen when you open your mind and allow the right person (or pony) to have a look in

A familiar backstory?

As I've mentioned, I was brought up in the 1980s. Even for those who weren't born, it's a decade that evokes heaps of nostalgia as a simpler time when it was great to be a child: the cartoons, the movies, the early computer games, even the sugar-rush inducing breakfast cereals. It easily conjures up feelings of security and innocence; it feels like a world away from the intense algorithmic headfuck of the social media age.

Yet for me, and I'm sure for many of my millennial readers, being young at that time also meant growing up in an emotional vacuum. There was a lack of warmth and encouragement from parents, and a lack of conversations about how we, as children, felt, and how the world around us worked. If we asked questions, "Because I said so" or "Don't be so stupid" were often the answer. We were also perhaps the last generation for whom excessive physical punishment was generally deemed acceptable. (Some countries have thankfully managed to outlaw such practices, although they are sadly still prevalent in others).

This might sound familiar: I grew up in a single-parent household (with an orbiting step-father showing up now and then) from an early age. When I was seven years old, I suffered what I now know to be my first panic attack: I got unexplainable stomach cramps during a gym session and I thought I was being swallowed by the ground.

Also, like many others, I learned to cope with my uncomfortable feelings by being on-the-go at all times and constantly keeping myself distracted. I joined my local ice hockey team, who had a busy and demanding schedule of training and regional league games. I loved the game and dreamed of a possible professional future. For the most part, however, it simply kept my mind occupied and my body moving. Then, when I was 13, a teammate died suddenly during a game. He was 14 years old.

None of us on the team, including those who witnessed the tragedy, received any counselling. No one checked if we were okay or how it might have affected us. My teammate's death made no sense to me, and although I couldn't share it with anyone, I became very worried about the briefness of life and the abruptness with which death could strike anyone, even healthy teenagers. This event triggered my next bouts of panic attacks. And this time, they were much stronger.

Although everything appeared fine on the outside, my mental health continued to erode during my teenage years, and once I started college, this began to manifest itself in further physical symptoms. I still had panic attacks (particularly around social situations), and then I began getting heart palpitations that left me convinced I was having a heart attack.

I sought help for my extreme physical symptoms. GPs sent me to have ECGs and CT scans. No one could find anything 'wrong' with me, but I still felt locked into a constant state of danger.

In my mid-teens, I started playing in bands, and then I started DJing. This was a great period of my life, but it was also exhausting. I would DJ anything up to 6 nights a week, and this of course entailed a lot of late nights, loads of drinking, plenty of partying, and just about getting through my higher education. This was, of course, balanced out by constant hangovers and fatigue that I would drink and party my way out of. Eat, sleep, feel like death, rave, repeat.

Normalising mental health, from the wrong direction

It would be another 25 years before I worked out that, throughout my childhood and all the way to my late twenties, I was in fact suffering from panic attacks and acute anxiety. Neither I nor the world around me were in tune with mental health, let alone how to fix it when issues arose. Any feelings that there was something wrong were quickly beaten down, and I certainly had no sense that anyone else could have been going through the same thing. After a while, it simply became a normal part of life. And this is what we so easily do, so much of the time. We get used to the aches, we adapt to the pain, we keep papering over the cracks. But it doesn't have to be that way.

The socially accepted form of self-medication that is alcohol was my vice and helper for many years. It helped mask my issues, all of which would make me uncomfortable in social situations. A few beers and I'd soon relax and feel a little more validated and accepted (not to mention funnier). But there are never any answers at the bottom of the glass. When I started seeing my friends graduate to self-medication through their noses and veins, I knew I had to distance myself from their presence. I had enough on my plate already.

As my creative business took off, that too became a means of escaping reality. As you've seen, I worked long and hard — and I kept it up for many years. It was gratifying, and through it I built a strong reputation and financial stability, but I did it all by turning a blind eye to the damage it was doing to my mind and body. Again, it didn't give me the answers I was subconsciously seeking. My issues were still unresolved

Need the nudge?

When something essential breaks, we generally fix it. Blown a tyre on your car or bike? Change it. Lightbulb gone? Batteries flat? Quickly sorted. This extends to our physical health: a sprained wrist, a broken ankle, a chipped tooth, a pulled muscle. All of these we attend to almost immediately because, particularly in the most severe cases, carrying on as before becomes impossible.

So why don't we approach mental health in the same way? Well, for a start, we are often very good at either hiding, justifying, or plain not noticing when something is amiss. Remember, we creatives excel at convincing others that we can do it all — and sometimes that means we can convince everyone, including ourselves, that we can do the entirety of life unaided. Work hard and play hard on a few hours' sleep and a can of Red Bull? Nailed it, mate.

Sometimes then, we need a nudge. We need something or someone to be gently honest with us and maybe suggest some healthy solutions before things get any worse. Untended mental issues always force themselves to a head; they're the leaking tap that eventually causes the bathroom ceiling to collapse. But it doesn't have to be a big dramatic event that causes it; sometimes, something far more mundane pushes you over the edge. In my case, I went to cross the street one day and found I couldn't do it. I went into a panic and anxiety attack so severe that I thought I was going to die.

This was the point at which the obstacles I'd been dodging for years hit me like an avalanche. It was time to make a change. However, it took Rachel suggesting therapy for me to go down that route. Had she not been there, I would likely have persevered down a non-therapy-based route, certain that I could somehow dig myself out of the hole I was in.

Taking action

I started getting counselling, and one of the first methods I was introduced to was Cognitive Behavioural Therapy (CBT). This is one of the baseline methods of therapy. In essence, you learn to observe your feelings and behaviours in certain situations and then, without judgement, record your thoughts, how they made you feel (both mentally and physically), and how you behaved as a result. So, someone doing CBT for anger management might record a situation where the red mist descended. They will look at the thoughts and physical sensations that arose (and how strong they were on a scale of, say, 1–10) and how they reacted as a result. Through doing this, triggers can be identified and worked on. It sounds simple to the point of banality, but if you've never done it, then it can be incredibly revealing, like cleaning a dirty window and seeing things clearly for the first time in ages. My CBT involved getting myself to cross a bridge (an actual bridge, not a metaphorical one), as I felt too anxious to do so. When my therapist suggested this for my first 'homework' assignment, I looked at her blankly and nearly asked, "Where are the pills to make this go away?"

Seeing things is one thing. Doing something about them is another. My first therapist also got me to audit my work, rest, and play ratios. They were totally out of whack. There was no way I could physically continue the way I had been, but I needed support. Rachel was a great help and kept nudging me to make changes. So that I had to leave the house, she even got me a dog, Hendrix (as in the sky-kissing guitar legend, not the upmarket gin or the character from Mad Men).

Such outside support and new kinds of new behaviours are vital because if nothing changes, then nothing changes. The ripple effect doesn't happen when you stare at the water and keep the stone in your hand; you have to throw it in. There has to be action

Accepting what you cannot change

After the first few months of counselling, I felt I was on the mend, but then my counsellor threw me a curveball by telling me that I would never be able to 'get my ducks fully in a row' (i.e., always be prepared for anything life threw at me). I reacted with shock. More than that, I found I was livid. Despite my progress, my counsellor had recognised that, deep down, I was still holding on to a naïve belief that I could somehow override (and therefore not have to deal with) human nature and our hardwired instincts.

This is something that is easily done when we seek therapy

Mindful Creative

or try to affect changes. There can be an inner resistance, our ego clinging on to catastrophic thoughts and romanticising the old days: "Yes, your life was a mess, but it was fun!" Sometimes it can win, too: think of the person who goes vegan on New Year's Eve. By the 3rd of January, they've convinced themselves that they can still have one little harmless bit of dairy every now and again. By the middle of January, they're eating more meat and dairy than ever. The mental gymnastics involved in this kind of resistance to change can be so subtle that we hardly notice it, and it can be an unpleasant shock to have it pointed out to us.

But when we've fallen into negative mental and physical habits because we seek control, then true change can only come when we accept that we cannot control everything, not events, not other people, not even our own thoughts. All we can have control over is how we react to those events. We have that much power. It may not seem like much when put that way, but it's a hell of a lot more than we have when we're rushing around trying to stop the tide coming in with a bucket

Therapy is a journey, not an operation

Despite some bumps in the road, I continued to make positive changes over the weeks, months, and eventually years. I became physically and mentally healthier (the two are always linked) and worked on getting rid of my unhealthy thinking patterns: I stopped being so blinded by my career and dragged myself away from relying on social media for validation. Unexpectedly, I then began to unravel my childhood through therapy.

Realising how the mind became hardwired the way it did during my formative years has had a massive impact on every area of my life. And just like everyone else who goes through the same thing, I'd spent decades blissfully unaware of it. On the contrary, we often wear our mentality with pride and think it's everyone else that needs fixing. Therapy can help us uncover these issues in our mental circuitry. It can also give us the right tools to begin fixing them

Therapy for everything and everyone...

During the last ten years, I have had different kinds of therapy for a range of issues. When parenthood hit me and Rachel (if you've been there, you know), we did couples therapy and helped to work through many issues that had come up that I wasn't even aware of. During the pandemic, my anxiety flared up, particularly around mortality and my ability to be there for my kids in case I happened to be one of the casualties of the virus. I did anxiety coaching, which is a form of therapy that focuses on setting and achieving goals more than healing past trauma. Through this, I was able to begin cultivating a more (self-)compassionate mindset, which, once you've got it, can become a life-saving self-care method and can totally change how you see and view other people. You're less likely to see everyone as a threat or an enemy, or see their actions as being directed against you.

At the time of writing, equine therapy is the most recent form of therapy, and like all of the others, it has helped me immeasurably in ways that I could never have foreseen. It helped me to put all of the previous years' findings in perspective and make sense of it all.

Therapy has changed my life for the better, and I'm so glad that I was able to open myself up to it. If anything in my pre-therapy story resonates with you, then I cannot recommend professional help highly or urgently enough. The therapies I've undertaken are particular to my needs, and there is something out there that will suit you and your unique situation. The list is potentially endless — if you can imagine it, it's likely a form of therapy. It ranges from the cerebral (Acceptance and Commitment Therapy (ACT), counselling, etc.) to the practical (art therapy, colour therapy, dance therapy, etc.) There's therapy for individuals, couples, and groups. You can have sessions in person or online. It's an entire world, and if you let it and you work at it, it can help you with anything

...And that includes you

In a way, all of this seems kind of amusing because I never saw myself as an ill person, even though I ticked all the boxes. There are millions of people who endured far worse childhoods than I did, but it's all relative, and the sufferings of others shouldn't be some kind of yardstick you beat yourself with because you think you shouldn't – or don't deserve – to feel the way you do.

Therapy has clearly had a huge and positive impact on my life at a very deep level. But so what? Why have I shared my story with you? I've done so because therapy is one of the, if not the supreme, examples of letting other people into your private world and letting them help you. If we're struggling with things, or have buried our issues under tons of excess, then it's eventually going to impact our creativity. And as we've seen, the knock-on effect is that therapy can also help with your creativity. If you pick the right therapist for you, someone who understands where you're coming from both as a human being and as a creative, and if you let them in, then they can benefit you in untold ways.

They can challenge deeply held assumptions you may not even have realised you had; they can give you guidance on what to do when you hit a creative block; they can help you with strategies for building resilience; they can be a brilliantly objective observer, not necessarily of the work you create, but of the you that's doing the creating.

In that sense, they are a little like a sympathetic mechanic with a car: they can get under the hood and show you which parts of your engine need some loving attention.

"What happens is not as important as how you react to what happens."

Ellen Glasgow

Pages

132—163

Chapter - no.6

Mindful

Chapter - no.6

Mindful

Adopting a mindful approach means working to inhabit each present moment and using all of our inbuilt senses to process exactly what's happening. It helps you to see the world anew, putting first-person narratives aside and instead inviting a more richly detailed perspective. When we actively work to become more present, we engage our minds and discover more creative ways of navigating the world. In turn, our stress levels drop and our anxieties become more manageable. Creative blocks become less frequent, and when they do arrive, they're less scary. By helping us see things more clearly as they are, mindfulness aids the way we retain memories and shows us the little things that have helped us get to where we are. Those insights then help us sharpen our vision of the future — a future we feel more positive about.

When we cnd up in the same mess for the fourteenth time, we can long for things to be different. But the change can ultimately only come from us. We have to start making changes from within. It's important to note, however, that if there are bigger, much longer-term issues at play, then the techniques suggested here won't resolve them. Trying to manage years of emotional shutdown, negative habits, and/or non-existent self-care with one round of a breathing exercise is like putting a sticking plaster on a broken bone.

The methods here are tools for countering stress and overwhelm in the present moment, giving us the space we need to regroup. If used regularly, they can contribute to building resilience and good mental and physical habits in your everyday life. They are small steps that can beget giant steps, but if there's a deeper constant that underpins recurring stress or burnout, then these methods have to exist alongside therapy to be fully effective.

Awareness

This section is designed to help you find peace and clarity through the non-judgemental observation of what's happening in your inner and outer worlds. The ability to tune in to your own breath and connect it to your body is the first step in enabling you to find meaningful experiences in any number of situations throughout your day. It's also a tool that can rescue us from immediate panic and help us move forwards.

Such awareness is obviously more enjoyable (and therefore easier to do) when things are going well, and when we're happy, calm, and creative. It feels like the sun is shining, and it's so much simpler in those instances to lean back in your chair and say,

"I'm feeling good. This is how life should be all the time!"

Ironically, it can become much more difficult to do when the stress kicks in — i.e., when it's most beneficial. When bad things happen, the familiar thought patterns, physical sensations, and reactions can grab you, and before you know where you are, you've temporarily lost the ability to read the present moment.

In those instances, the only constructive way back, however much your old natural reactions want you not to, is to tune in and become aware of what's happening in your mind and your body. You can't always control what's happening around you, but you always have the power to control how you react to it.

The effect of tuning in is to step out of your thoughts and feelings and understand them for what they really are. We are great at creating our own versions of reality, which are often very different from how others might be seeing the same situation. Being caught up in a hurricane of anxious, stressful, or even angry thoughts is one thing.

Acknowledging that you are feeling anxious, stressed, or angry and noticing how those thoughts are making your body feel is another. Even if you're hyperventilating, realising that you're hyperventilating is one step removed from thinking that you're dying. And it's that step, however small, that we can take to begin working our way back to our baseline

Understanding negative patterns

The kinds of negative patterns that lead to moments of intense stress, anxiety, overwhelm, or even total burnout aren't some kind of one-off pop-up in your mind; they're an established chain that has cemented its presence in your mind over time, and which can chip away at your resilience.

When we can learn to recognise and chart these patterns, including the mental and physical reactions that they generate, then we can begin working to notice them when they crop up. If we stick at it, then we can counter them more quickly and get back into a more positive inner groove. Think of it like weeding your garden path or your driveway. Pulling weeds up as soon as they sprout won't stop weeds from ever growing again, but it will stop them from taking over.

The power of what you already possess

You already own everything you need to begin practising mindful awareness: your breath and your mind. Your breath is the tool with which you can begin to (re)build your baseline of mindful presence, no matter how far out of the present moment you've ended up and no matter how often you find yourself astray.

Let's look at some essential ways to build and reinforce your mindful baseline. If any of them feel a little tricky to grasp or follow unguided, then meditation apps are available for extra support.

However, they aren't a necessity; you can start in the simplest way imaginable: by either sitting or lying down and doing gentle breathing exercises, such as those outlined below. When you tune into your breath, you begin to become aware of the present moment and what's going on in and around you.

Breathing exercises

Here are three simple breathing exercises for creatives that you can incorporate into your daily routine. You only need a chair and 10 minutes where you won't be disturbed. The first is a breathing exercise for presence, the second is a body scan, and the third is a meditation for gaining space in the mind. As you'll see, they all operate on the same basic principles of sitting, breathing, and noticing. Audio versions of each are available by following the link at the end of this book.

Breathing exercise no.1

This is a very simple exercise for tuning into your breath that requires as little as a couple of minutes per day — and the maximum benefits will come from doing it every day. You can do it on your sofa, sat at your desk, and you can even modify it so that you can do it when you're walking down the road or waiting in a queue.

Wherever you do it, it's a fantastic anchor for bringing us into the present. The more you can do it every day, the more natural it will become, and the more it will become habit.

— Find a comfortable place to sit where you can be undisturbed for about 10 minutes. Feel free to use a chair, sitting with both feet on the floor. Alternatively, you can sit cross-legged on your bed or on the floor. Either way, keep your back relaxed and supported.

— Gently close your eyes and start to take in any sounds that are around you. The sounds will change and come and go. That's no problem. Just notice that they're there and be content to keep them in the background.

— Begin to notice how you're breathing — don't change it, just notice it; cast your mental gaze on the breath. Notice how it feels as you breathe in, where in your body the breath travels to, its rhythm, its pace, and how it feels as it leaves the body.

— Settle into this inner gazing and keep your relaxed, curious attention on your breathing for a few minutes.

— If the mind becomes distracted by thoughts or sounds, that's okay; it's perfectly natural. Gently bring your attention back to your breath.

— When you're ready, slowly take a deep breath in, filling your lungs and belly. Hold your breath for a second, then slowly exhale in three parts:

— Exhale a little, then pause.
— Exhale a little more, then pause again.
— Then finally, exhale fully and completely.
— Allow the breath to return to normal.

— Do this intentional, incremental breathing two more

times. Breathing in slowly, fully, deeply, and exhaling in three increments, pausing between each one.

— With each exhalation, notice how your body also drops further into the seat, how your shoulders let go a little, and how the muscles gradually surrender any tension.

— After three rounds of incremental exhalation, let your breathing fully return to normal for a couple of minutes, resting with the familiarity and comfort of its gentle rhythm.

— Slowly bring yourself back to the space that you're in. Notice the sounds around you, the feel of the air on your skin.

— Take a deep breath in, slowly let it out, and gently open your eyes. How do you feel?

A simple breathing exercise like this slows us right down, brings us into the present, and helps ground our attention fully in this moment

Body scan no.2

Body scan exercises are another great way of bringing your minds into the present and anchoring them there. By starting at the top of your head and methodically working down to your toes, paying attention to each part of the body and every sensation you feel, you can interrupt any mental chatter and calm both your mind and body. Sometimes you might feel a lot; other times you might not feel anything. Both are equally valid. Observing what you do or don't find without judgement is what's important here.

— Sit somewhere comfortable with your back straight and your hands in your lap.

— Close your eyes, take a long deep breath in and slowly let it out.

— Settle a little deeper into the seat, feeling its full support.

— Start to notice how your head is feeling today, whether it's feeling heavy or sitting lightly on your neck.

— With the same gentle curiosity, notice any sensations on your face. Is there any tension in your jaw, or the little muscles around your eyes or lips? Don't attempt to change anything you find, just observe.

— Next, consider any sensations in your neck and shoulders. Are they sore and tight or loose and light?

— Bring your mental gaze down to your chest and upper back, scanning for any sensations or differences in temperature. Perhaps there won't be much to notice, and that's okay too. We're here with no expectations, only curiosity.

— If you become distracted by thoughts or sounds, that's okay; it happens all the time. Bring your attention back to the body.

— Observe the arms and any feelings in your hands and fingertips, whether there's any tingling or currents of energy.

— Bring your awareness to your belly and hips, your lower back, and your sitting bones, feeling the contact of the seat with your body.

— Observe how your thighs feel, and then the fronts and backs of your knees.

— Send your attention down to your shins and calves, then down to your ankles, feet, and toes. Notice where your feet touch the floor.

— Now consider your whole body and all the sensations you've felt, how they're so different in different parts of your body.

— Expand your awareness to the space just a couple of inches away from your body, the space that's holding your body.

Feel the space and the wholeness of this space that your body inhabits.

— Finally, take a deep breath in, feeling the breath travel down through your whole body, through your spine and legs, and then gently breathe out.

— Notice how you feel in your body now. And in your own time, gently open your eyes and come back to the room

Make space ᴺᴼ.3

This is a simple meditation to make some space in your mind, a space from which new creative inspiration and perspectives may emerge. It takes around 10 minutes.

— Sit with your back upright and relaxed, your hands loose in your lap.

— Take a moment to look at the space around you, noticing the room, and then gently close your eyes.

— Take one long, deep breath in, and then exhale slowly and fully, dropping the shoulders as you do so. Arrive fully in the moment.

— Let the breath flow naturally and observe it for a little while.

— Become an observer, watching what thoughts are in your mind at this time. Sometimes when we do this, it goes empty — we don't find any thoughts. If that's what happens, then dwell there, in the vast spaciousness.

— Other times, you might find an endless stream of thoughts running through your mind one after another, or all at once, or one persistent thought refusing to go away. Whatever happens, become a silent witness, watching thoughts float past like clouds in the sky of your mind. Let them come and go. Don't hold on to them or get carried away by them. If that does happen, simply return to observing.

— Whatever thoughts you find yourself watching, imagine them to be like clouds — let them dissipate as if they were turning into rain and falling to the earth, leaving a clear blue sky.

— Rest in the spaciousness of the mind. Any urgent thoughts can wait until after the practice.

— Bring your attention to your body, starting with the head. Imagine that all heaviness and busy-ness is draining from your head, down through your body, and out into the earth at your feet.

— Bring your awareness to your neck and shoulders and imagine your muscles and joints loosening, almost as if they're coming apart from your body. Feel the space and lightness in this area.

— Notice the upper body and lower body and the arms. And once again, if there is any tension or tightness, imagine it all draining down through your body, through your feet, onto the floor, and becoming absorbed by the earth.

— Allow this same letting go in your hips and legs, feeling all tension fall downwards into the earth.

— Finally, feel the contact of your feet with the floor, as the last residue of any tension or worry flows through them and out of your body.

— Now imagine a warm, white light just above the top of your head. Imagine this light is flowing down through your head and down through your body and limbs — every inch of your body is radiating with this light.

— Stay here in this spaciousness, this lightness, this clarity, from which creativity may flow.

— As the light is slowly absorbed into your body, it starts to fade, leaving the sense of spaciousness.

— Keeping this sense of spaciousness with you, slowly start to come back to the space around you, hearing the sound of your breathing and feeling the contact of the seat with your body, feeling the temperature and texture of the air around you, and noting any sounds you can hear.

— When you're ready, take a deep breath in and out, and gently open your eyes

Alternative breathing exercises

There are many other techniques you can use when you're not able to set aside time for a mindfulness meditation. Whether you're on a train platform, or in a packed train carriage, you can use these techniques to bring your mind back to your baselines or tackle a situation that appeared out of nowhere. A few of these include:

— **Square breathing** (also known as Box Breathing and 4x4 Breathing): This is where you breathe in slowly through your nose whilst counting to four. You then hold your breath for another count of four and then exhale for a further count of four. Hold your breath again for a count of four and repeat the whole process for a few minutes or as long as necessary

— **4-7-8 breathing** (also known as Relaxing Breathing): This is a similar technique to Square Breathing, but the counts are different. You inhale for a count of four, hold your breath for a count of seven, and then exhale for a count of eight (making a whooshing noise as you do so). Then the process starts over.

— **Deep breathing** (also known as Diaphragmatic Breathing): To do deep breathing, sit up with your back straight or lie down on the floor. Place one hand on your abdomen and one on your chest. Breathe in slowly and deeply through your nose and feel your abdomen rise. Exhale slowly through your mouth and feel your abdomen fall. Throughout, focus your concentration on the rise and fall of your abdomen.

— **Pursed-lip breathing:** This method involves breathing in through your nose for a count of two, feeling your stomach expand, and then pursing your lips (imagine you're going to blow on a hot cup of coffee) and gently breathing out for a count of four (or at least for longer than you breathed in).

— **Alternate nostril breathing:** This is a technique sometimes found in yoga. Sitting up, you close your right nostril with your right thumb and breathe in through your left nostril. You then close your left nostril with your right ring finger and exhale through your right nostril. You then inhale through your right nostril, close it with your thumb, and exhale through your left nostril. You then repeat the process.

— **Breath counting:** Here, you simply breathe in gently but fully through your nose and exhale deeply through your mouth, each in-and-out representing one breath. Mentally count each breath up to 10, and then start counting from one again. If you realise that you've been distracted and lost count, then don't judge yourself for it, simply start again from one.

You may find one technique works for you more than the others, so it's worth trying different ones and finding your best fit. The key is repetition and consistency. Learning to use mindful breathing effectively takes time and practise. You're building a strong inner muscle to help you cope with whatever comes your way.

Making time and space for progress

The important thing to remember when doing these kinds of exercises, no matter how often you do them, is that no level of perfection can be attained. It doesn't exist. Your mind will always drift off and it will always be generating thoughts. Sometimes these thoughts may be busier than others, and sometimes you might be wishing for a positive outcome that might not be there at that moment. Mindful breathing and meditations are your ways of moving forward. And just like you might have a bad run of creative work or a not-so-good day at the gym, it's never guaranteed to work right from the start. Either way, the mind will always be churning endless thoughts about your progress, until one day, you'll let go and simply be with your thoughts and your stillness. When you find yourself battling your thoughts and judgements, all you need to do is to recognise that your mind is straying and gently return your attention to your breath and the present moment.

There is no deadline to meet with mindful breathing, and it's not a race. This is a practice that you get to build in your own time and at your own speed. As you continue to do it, so you will begin to feel its benefits.

You'll find yourself able to cope with stressful situations more effectively; you'll be able to catch your negative patterns that little bit quicker; you'll begin to make better decisions about how you react to everything in your life.

You can gain the full effects of breathing exercises by doing them regularly and building them into your routine. This might mean waking up 10 minutes earlier in the morning to do your preferred guided breathing technique. It's a small change that will start adding up over time.

The mindful breathing techniques should help you ground your feelings and emotions before any tricky or stressful task. You don't even have to sit and do a 10-minute breathing exercise; you can simply pause, take a breath, and bring yourself into the present moment.

Think how a footballer about to take a penalty kick pauses, takes a breath, and considers where they're going to aim the ball. They might not hit the target every time, but they stand a better chance than if they blindly smack the ball as hard as possible and hope for the best.

Self-understanding and acceptance

Throughout all of this, please remember that I'm not telling you to be like me, or like anyone else. Where I've used examples of others, it's as an illustration of the power of someone who has adopted mindful techniques to bring out the best in them. The difference between being inspired by someone and emulating them is subtle but crucial. Just because someone appears zen AF to us, it doesn't mean they're like that all of the time. And besides, we might be making up yet another story in our minds that we're failing to be just like them. Once again, our interpretation isn't necessarily a true reflection of reality.

We can be inspired by how we want to be to others and use that inspiration to become the best version of ourselves. And we can be inspired by anyone, it can be peers, partners, friends, co-workers, and even (or maybe especially) our children.

What's more, we can use that kind of inspiration most effectively when we understand and accept ourselves; when we know our strengths and weaknesses and don't fight them, ignore them, or belittle them. This is where therapy and coaching can help you to bring out the best version of yourself

Understanding our thoughts

I mentioned above that our thoughts are always going to be there; our minds will never be short of them. Some thoughts are positive, some are negative, and some are intrusive.

Positive thoughts can come in the form of affirmations

(reminding yourself of your strengths and good qualities), compassionate thoughts (showing kindness and understanding to yourself and others), gratitude (being grateful for things, however big or small), and constructive problem solving (looking for helpful solutions).

Negative thoughts can involve catastrophising (imagining worst-case scenarios or believing that things are bound to go wrong somehow), overgeneralising (assuming a negative outcome because of an isolated incident), irrationally harsh self-criticism (which can lead to you mislabelling yourself as an 'idiot' or a 'failure', etc.), and rumination (a destructive version of problem solving that keeps dwelling on past mistakes and regrets, seeking answers that cannot be found).

The mind is often described as a big 'what if?' machine, and for many people, that's okay; negative thoughts come and go largely unnoticed. But for others, it can feel like certain unwanted thoughts get trapped in a revolving door and go round and round. These intrusive thoughts can sometimes go beyond the negative and become terrifyingly dark. When these thoughts come up — and they can arise at any time and be triggered by seemingly trivial things — they can seem very real, but it's important to remember that they are only thoughts; they're not reality and they don't define you. Moreover, you're far from the only person to have them.

When dealing with negative thinking, the key to countering it is not to stop it — thoughts can't be turned off the way you can turn your television off — but to acknowledge its presence and then let the thought pass on its way without tying yourself to it.

Thoughts arise out of the ether. If you don't engage with them, then they'll go back into the ether. The more you try to fight them, the more they become like an invasive door-to-door salesperson who jams their foot in the door when you try to close it. However, if you hear them knocking, don't answer the door, and don't engage with them, they'll soon go away. Mindful practices, such as breathing exercises, journaling, and CBT can help you to understand, accept, and manage your thinking and how it may affect you and your health and wellbeing. When these methods don't work and negative and/or intrusive thoughts continue to be overwhelming, then professional therapy is there to help you.

Whilst all kinds of thoughts will always be there, your thought process can often be teased in a more positive direction when you objectively understand your thoughts and make peace with both them and the things you're thinking about. If you're constantly battling everything around you, then your mind is more likely to remain stuck in a fighting, victim mindset that sees everything as a grim struggle towards a victory that won't make you happy. If you accept how the day has gone and find the positives, and if you make a habit of it, then your mind will more naturally seek the positives in any given situation. You will find yourself in touch with your mindful baseline more often. There will always be endless moments that can threaten to derail your baselines, but it's how you manage to react to them that will influence your overall mood, stress, and balance. Stressful situations, conflict, and negative thoughts exist to test our resilience and defence systems. This is why it's imperative to build a strong ability to deal with them as they arise

Understanding stress

In the way that our thoughts are a natural part of having a brain, stress is an inevitable part of being alive and in our bodies. Stress can be both positive and negative, and its different forms have names:

Positive stress is **eustress:** this is the kind of short-term, manageable stress that brings out the best in us; it can energise us and help us focus. It's the kind of stress we feel when the pressure's on but we can rise to it and we feel it's worth it. It's when someone tasks us with something and we feel that rush of excitement and say, "I'm on it".

Negative stress is **distress:** we may never have heard of eustress, but we all know what distress means. When stress in any situation (work, relationships, money worries, long-term illness, etc.) is prolonged and pushes us beyond our ability to cope, then it becomes distress, and it can have profound effects on our short- and long-term health: we can become depressed, upset, and even develop physical symptoms.

We are always going to find ourselves presented with stressful situations that may be of our own doing, the consequence of someone else's actions, or simply freakish bad luck. Either way, our stress response is always physical on some level, whether our brain sends us into fight, flight, or freeze. Knowing this and understanding how stress physically affects us is part of nurturing a mindful approach to our lives and work.

We can also gain insight into how well we cope with stress by remembering that we don't exist in a vacuum and that our stress response can affect those around us. This isn't an exercise in shaming ourselves; it's a way of being open to how others perceive us, and it can help us see ourselves in a new light. We might not realise that we become jumpy, snappy, or uncommunicative when we're stressed, or we might think that it's because we've had too much caffeine, but if someone can constructively point out how we behave when we're stressed, then we might feel a little embarrassed, but we'll ultimately get a new view of ourselves that we can use to build self-awareness. Stress is a natural part of life, more so today than ever, and particularly in creative lines of work, but not dealing with it consciously and productively can have huge impacts on our creativity and our physical and mental health. If nothing else, trying to cope with too much stress is exhausting on every level. When it first arises is the time we want to realise and use our mindful toolbox to head back to our baseline

Understanding the signal

So far, we've looked at ways to gain insight into ourselves. But we exist in a world with other people, all of whom have their own shit to deal with. We can't always understand how they're feeling and thinking by remaining totally self-absorbed. We might think we can understand, especially when we're so good at creating convincing backstories about other people and assigning all kinds of motives to them, but it's not the same thing as asking them. More than that, it's not the same thing as asking them and actually listening to what they say.

Our anxiety to be heard and to prove ourselves can sometimes run roughshod over our ability to actively listen to what someone is saying. We might be too busy formulating our own thoughts. We might be so keen to get our point of view across that we talk over others. We might assume we know what's in the other person's mind and attempt to end their sentences for them. Our ego and intelligence are pushing to the forefront at the expense of our focus. Mindful presence and practice can counter these urges, which can sometimes be so hardwired that we don't even realise we're doing them. They can help us to hear what is being said, pause, and think before we reply. We always have the power to listen and then say that we don't understand, or even that we don't agree — even to not have an opinion, which is perhaps an even more empowering stance in our increasingly hot-take, opinion-driven, social-media society.

Being interested in fully understanding what others have to say, be it clients, friends, family, or podcast guests, can teach you new things, help to broaden your horizons, check your preconceptions, and cultivate the compassion that naturally arises from a more mindful approach to life. You become more curious about and more aware of why a person might do or say what they do; you'll realise that (and I mean this in a positive way) not everything is about you; everyone is trying to navigate thoughts and stress just like you.

Being interested and compassionate doesn't necessarily mean that you agree with what another person says or that you shouldn't challenge it or ask for clarity, but you can only truly work out whether you agree or understand or not by knowing yourself and being in the present moment and listening

Other useful tools

As well as breathing and listening, there are other useful and impactful tools you can employ at a moment's notice to help bring you back into your body and the present moment. They can be done at any time during the day and they are all easy.

— Find the time to step away from your desk (or wherever you're working) at regular intervals. Take a walk around. If it's a nice day, go outside and feel the air. If you work at home and you've got a garden, go and feel the grass underneath your feet.

— When you're away from your desk to make a cup of tea, have lunch, or even go to the toilet, take some gentle breaths and roll your shoulders backwards and forwards a couple of times.

— Make space to read or listen to a book or podcast and aim to spend those moments, however few, as emerged in t he story or conversation as you can. If any frenetic thoughts try to push into your cognitive space, simply observe them and rerun the podcast or reread the page of the book again.

— Yoga and Pilates classes can work miracles for your physical and mental flexibility. If you're unable to get out to a class, there are dozens of worthwhile YouTube channels out there with yoga for just about anything you can think of. They can be an hour long; they can be five minutes. They can be gentle; they can be intense. Try some and see which suits you.

— If there's a certain yoga or Pilates stretch that you find particularly restorative and which pulls you back to(wards) your baseline, then don't wait for class; do it now! Do it a few times a day whenever you get chance. You can't return to the present moment enough

Keep checking back

Monitoring your progress and taking positives from it is a brilliant way to nudge your thoughts into a healthy overall direction. When you compare how you react to a stressful situation after a few weeks or months of practising mindfulness, you might be pleasantly surprised to find out how much better you handle things. And, of course, those around you will be benefiting too.

As your ability and willingness to return to the present moment increases, it becomes less likely that you'll vanish down rabbit holes of overwhelm and distraction so easily — your focus will improve, making you more productive (in the healthiest sense of the word) and more creative. Coming back to the now more often also means that you're less likely to feel you haven't got enough time for everything.

In short, you'll become a creative athlete, constantly building your healthiest habits, always turning up, and making the right kinds of small efforts to succeed in your discipline and life

It takes as long as it takes

The final thing to remember is that everything mentioned here takes time. If you're totally new to the techniques mentioned here, you're not going to have them licked by next Tuesday, or even the Tuesday after that. Despite our speed-and-results driven society, it's crucial to approach everything mentioned in this section with the understanding that:

— None of it can be perfected, only constantly practised.

— It all takes as long as it takes.

To reiterate: the techniques suggested here are not sticking plasters; they're approaches you can adopt to gradually improve your state of mind and therefore your approach to your business and creative practices. They make life easier, but they take constant effort until they become habit. They are also far deeper than I've been able to cover here. You can find entire books, lectures, and courses devoted only to active listening or mindful breathing.

This book is a map pointing out possible destinations, not the destination itself.

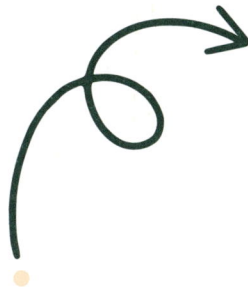

"Nothing can harm you as much as your own thoughts unguarded."

Buddha

Pages

164–185

Chapter - no.7

Positive habits

Chapter - no.7

<u>170.</u> Mood defines action
(and affects changes)
<u>171.</u> The importance of planning
and not multitasking
<u>173.</u> *Asking for help and clarity*
<u>174.</u> Time to appraise
your progress
<u>175.</u> *"Have you had your
Mars bar yet?"*

177. Become easily un-stuck
179. *Start where
it makes sense*
180. Dare to take time off
181. *Learn to say no*
182. Smile on
the inside
183. Keeping positive habits

Positive habits

So you've got to the place where you're able to take a breath and root yourself in the present moment. How do you take that ability and begin to build on it? How do you expand on it to positively affect your life and your creative practice and work past day-to-day issues such as creative blocks, procrastination, or even just waking up in a bit of a shitty mood? Equally as important, how do you use it to conquer your day — because if you don't control your day, someone else will happily do it for you. And not necessarily in a good way.

In that spirit, this section looks at some more small actions you can start taking right now. If you can turn them into habits, then they will help you move much bigger boulders further along the road.

Mood defines action (and affects change)

Three people inspire me every day. Seeing them makes me get my act together. I don't know who they are, and I don't know their names. All I know is that they're my superheroes, and they wear running shoes. Every morning, they run past my window, regardless. Mud everywhere? No problem. Sub-zero temperatures? They might have stuck some gloves on. I like running too (albeit not as much as they seem to), but that's not what inspires me. What is re-affirmed for me every time I see them go jogging past is the validity of taking constant action.

Often, our actions and mood can operate in a feedback loop, one helping to determine the other. If we feel positive, we'll take positive action, and the more we do the positive action, the more likely it is that we'll feel more positive (and so continue to do the action). But there are always so many factors at play that are beyond our control: we might get bad feedback or not win a contract, someone in a shop might be rude to us for no reason, and it's those times, when we feel down or angry or lethargic, that are the danger zones. It's when we can so easily slip back into bad habits. We can start scrolling, bingeing, catastrophising, and so on.

Yet it's precisely those times that we can also use our ability to pause, recognise that we're not feeling our best, and then basically force ourselves to do something about it. We can't fight the elements, but we can challenge ourselves. I'm sure there's at least one morning a week where one of my three heroes can't be bothered and wants to hit snooze or stay in the warm, but I'd never know which one or when because they always show up.

Sometimes you've just got to force yourself up and off your sofa or out of your bed or out of the doldrums and crack on.

You'll notice that I said 'do something about it' in the last paragraph, and that's deliberate because there's a kind of small-print attached to taking positive actions. When we're not at our best, they're not guaranteed to make us feel better, but they certainly increase the chances. You've got to be in it to win it

The importance of planning and not multitasking

We touched on the importance of planning in the previous section, and it's worth restating because it can so often get forgotten when we think we can just veer off quickly and do this one little thing, or let ourselves off not doing something and so adding it on to tomorrow's to-do list, which we decide we don't need to write down because we can keep it all in our head. Tomorrow starts today is a bit of a cliché, but it's true: writing out tomorrow's to-do list, and then remembering to look at it and do the things on it, can be massively beneficial for our productivity and our state of mind.

When we're writing lists, however, and planning things that are off in the future, our old biases can kick in and make us think things will flow a lot more easily than they realistically will. If you've ever allocated 30 minutes for a drive that should take that long but always takes longer because of traffic, or if you've ever been drunk in the early hours and thought to yourself, "I feel great! I reckon I might get up at six and go for a run!", then you'll know what I mean. It's very useful to know yourself and be honest about your habits when it comes to planning. Are you most creative first thing? Plan to do the bulk of your work then. A natural night-owl? That's great. Work to that if you wish — although it might put you out of sync with the rest of your family or friends. Getting the work done isn't often about being the most inspired; it's the planning and optimal conditions that help you cross the finishing line.

It's easier said than done, but aim to focus on one thing at a time and avoid the temptation to jump around from one unfinished task to another. We tend to regard multitasking as a superpower, and if you can keep all your plates spinning without any falling off, then you are indeed approaching superhero status. The bad news if you like that approach is that we lose the ability to overlap our multitasking as we get older. We become more focused and less distracted out of necessity rather than choice.

Of course, there are also times when multitasking is logical, even necessary — you wouldn't cook a Sunday roast one ingredient at a time — but generally speaking, we cannot give multiple tasks our attention simultaneously and stay in the present moment. If we're working but also have one eye across all of our social channels whilst also watching wannabe influencers wasting oxygen in their latest Netflix series on top of trying to plan what we're going to have for dinner later and when we should next go to the gym, then it can get dizzying, right?! We're clearly not going to be giving our work and our creative practice our full attention. Tasks get completed on autopilot and mistakes get made. Creative satisfaction is diluted and work often rushed.

You might never be able to get your ducks in a row, but you

should avoid having them two or three abreast. When you're at work, as much as possible, be at work and be doing the kind of work you have planned to do (if you're working a creative piece, don't think about your accounts and vice versa). When you're resting or playing, focus on that because those are the times your creative superpowers are recharging. Your subconscious is also busily looking for solutions to things you might be stuck on when you keep rolling them over in your conscious mind

Asking for help and clarity

If a creative task isn't explained or briefed right, you won't be able to do it right. If a brief is vague or over-complex, then you can find yourself guessing your way through. We can make a big issue of asking for help or clarity sometimes, feeling that to do so will make us look weak or stupid, or even worse, unprofessional.

But, let's face it, how likely are you to be belittled for emailing a client to clarify what they want? And what's better, doing that and getting the work right first time, or guessing wrong and losing precious time by making amendments? Why do star footballers on multi-million-pound contracts need a manager to keep them doing the right thing? We all need guidance and clarity.

Something similar can be said for when something is beyond your current skillset. If you can learn it, fantastic, but if it's an unrealistic ask, then there is always someone available to help you. It may cost a little money, but delegating out can buy back your time and ensure the work keeps running smoothly. You might even learn a thing or two. Ask for help and own it

Take time to appraise your progress

As well as marking out times of the day to look forwards, you can also mark out time to look back and appraise what you've done. We spoke about this when we looked at auditing your life. But it doesn't always have to be as rigorous as that. You can also gain insight and build resilience by taking a moment at the end of each day to reflect on how things have gone. There are even 'gratitude' apps that encourage you to write down a couple of things that have gone well before you go to bed.

If you're not used to speaking highly of yourself, always feeling that you have to couch any self-praise in self-deprecating humour, then this can appear daunting, maybe even painful. But it's not about blowing smoke up your own backside; it's about giving yourself valuable perspective on how you and your creativity and your business are progressing.

Getting something strong and sustainable up and running takes time, and yes, there are the shit jobs to work through, the mistakes to make, and the intrusive thoughts to challenge, but by constantly showing up with a plan, following it through, and then taking the time to recognise your little wins, you're putting yourself more in the way of opportunity and success than if you don't. There's nothing spiritual or metaphysical about that; it's simple logic. Who's likely the better runner? A person who goes for the odd run every now and then, or the three guys going past my window every morning?

"Have you had your Mars bar yet?"

Many moons ago, one of my projects included marketing collateral for a local Mexican restaurant. One of the secret perks of this was the vast number of printed vouchers for free nachos in exchange for an email address that was often simply made up. Oops. As you can imagine, I got through a few of the vouchers and nachos alike.

We can't hide the fact that an office diet isn't the healthiest of them all. We are all guilty of eating at our desks to save time on breaks in favour of maximising creative time. In fact, when one of the guys from the Mexican would come to collect the stuff we'd done for him, often during the lunchtime pick up, he'd always ask if we'd "had your Mars bar yet". It became a running joke how silly the lunch habits could appear to an outsider. He often backed up his joke with a free Mexican takeaway for us, delivered right to the office.

Now, having a sense of humour is indispensable (and we'll get to that shortly), but this banter was making light of the uncomfortable fact that we were fuelling ourselves with the wrong things. Unless you spend time and effort planning out your food with the right knowledge, you can fall into the broad bracket of office workers who survive largely on a diet of processed food, refined sugar, too much caffeine, and not enough water. It easily becomes a habit, partly in reaction to our environment and the stress we often put ourselves under. The giveaway is when your energy levels throughout a given day resemble a sine wave: up and down in big peaks and troughs.

Realising how intrinsically your diet is linked to your mood is a real game-changer. It feeds into the mood/action feedback loop we looked at earlier. Realising what food and drink suits you best, and at what time of day, can also invigorate your energy and sleep levels. It involves learning about yourself as much as learning about which foods are the healthiest. How you feel after you've eaten something can indicate whether you're doing it right or not.

If you want to become a creative athlete, and keep yourself strong, then there are some habits you can begin building. One of the most obvious concerns your diet. The right healthy food means a healthy body, which can contribute to a healthy mind and a healthy creative practice by giving you sustained levels of energy, not the sickly rollercoaster that energy drinks and chocolate bars chain you to.

Planning is vital. If you don't plan your workload right, you'll end up in a mess. If you don't make the time to prepare and enjoy your food properly, you'll end up rushing and grabbing whatever comes to hand (assuming you remember to eat at all).

If you've got a busy life, and especially if you've got kids, then taking 10-15 minutes before the start of each week to work out what you're going to eat each day can transform your diet. Make time for mealtimes where possible, or at least try and eat at roughly the same time every day. And remember to leave sufficient time to prepare your food beforehand.

Sometimes, we can be so preoccupied that we can eat a whole meal without noticing a single thing about it. When you eat, try and slow down. Focus on the smell, the taste, and the look of your food. Savour it as you chew. Even if you only manage to do this once a day, it's a way of becoming present. And the more you do it, the more natural it will become.

It's been scientifically proven that the more visually appealing food is, the better people think it tastes. So, bearing in mind that it's food that you're going to eat (and smell and look at and savour), try to make every meal the best it can be. Search for the colours and flavours that wake you up and which inspire your taste buds and your creativity. Share that inspiration by cooking for others.

There's no one more passionate about their craft as chefs at the top of their game. Their obsession with flavour and the essences of culinary creativity can be mind-blowing and immensely inspiring. Watch an episode of shows such as The Chef's Table or The Chef Show and take notes — mental, edible or otherwise. Even if you're no Michelin star chef, simple seasoning or cooking techniques can transform the most ordinary dish into something you'd happily pay good money for in a restaurant.

Becoming easily un-stuck

What happens when you decide to drive to a place you've never been before? Do you plan your journey meticulously or do you simply decide to set off and see how and when you get there? The lack of map and direction will easily get you into a few dead-ends and one-way streets, and will ultimately take much longer. It might be fun to get lost and see the unexpected sometimes, but it often doesn't work when time is in short supply — such as the moments we try to break through a creative block on a stressful deadline day.

Taking small steps of positive action can be really useful in confronting creative blocks — one of the creative's natural enemies. But what are creative blocks, beyond times when the ideas or the inspiration just won't come? They can be a mixture of a lack of mapped-out process, anxiety, and ego — a self-imposed lack of direction. That might sound a little harsh, but your creativity and your ideas ultimately have to come from within, so if you're sat there, unable to think of a good idea, then who else is stopping you from coming up with the idea except yourself?

Of course, some days, we feel naturally more in tune than others: the work just seems to flow and we can pluck genius ideas out of nowhere. But the times when that's not happening are the times when we can either sit there worrying and getting frustrated or start doing things to tune back in and put ourselves in inspiration's way. Positive, effective approaches are the key to getting yourself un-stuck every time — or even better, not getting stuck in the first place.

There are many ways this can be done, and most of them involve stepping away a little and engaging your mind in something else. It can be little things where you time out to have fun with your creativity, even doodling moustaches on celebrities in magazines or doing some automatic writing (just start writing without stopping to think about or analyse it).

You can step away from your work and go for a walk, or a run; you can go and read a chapter of a book or do a crossword or play an instrument. You can maybe even look back over some of your existing portfolio, anything that takes the pressure off and lets your mind have a wander. It's a positive way of expanding on pausing to take a breath, and it can help you to (re)discover pathways to solutions that are always there but just need finding

Start where it makes sense

writing in the middle of a sentence, it wouldn't make sense, would it? That's not a typo; it's showing you how confusing things can quickly appear if you start from an illogical place. But it's something that we can often end up doing, especially when we're in our element and our ideas are coming at us from all angles, often for a bit of work that we've yet to get to. And believe me, I know how easy it can be to suddenly find yourself down those rabbit-holes, not wanting to let the idea get away. And whilst it is positive and beautiful to have the flexibility to reach out and catch those ideas by noting them down, it's equally important that you can switch back into a logical course of action. Otherwise, your work can become like a drunken conversation, veering off on tangents to the point where you forget what you were originally talking about.

The easiest way to navigate this issue is always to start anything — your day, your work, even your rest and play — from a logical starting point. You might need to have some flexibility as to where that logical starting point might be on a given day, but breaking time and tasks down beforehand and planning out how you can most effectively employ your time and energy can get you on the good foot.

Starting this way can also help you to basically understand the work you're doing. Many of us have jumped straight into something before without reading the email or brief properly, only to find ourselves quickly getting confused. We have to stop and go back, and we lose valuable time. Sometimes the desire to act can be so strong that even stopping for a minute to take a breath can have our creative urges pulling at us like an impatient child, but when we've got into that space, even just using it to read something back to ourselves or listen to a voice note again can set us up for a much more focused and productive time.

Dare to take time off

One of the most positive things we can do for ourselves and our work is to take a holiday every now and then. This isn't about earning or deserving anything; it's about you having the right to rest and recharge your batteries. Your health, work, family, friends, and colleagues will all benefit. To some people, this will be obvious; but to others, it will be an alien concept.

Taking a break — hitting the off switch hard — can instantly lift a weight off our shoulders and help us to see things differently. Yet sometimes, whether we're our own boss or we work for someone else, it can sometimes feel wrong to swan off for a week, or even a day. My wife eventually had to force me to have a day off. But why is this? It can be many things, but it can often come down to fear: if we stop working, if we're not there to answer the call or reply to the email straight away, then it's all over. Deadlines will get missed, clients won't come back, bills won't get paid, etc. etc.

So, yes, sometimes we have to dare ourselves to take a day off. We have to learn to trust that downing tools for a short period of time won't signal the end of life as we know it. And in all honesty, the world will be able to cope without us being in the office for a few days every now and again. You're taking time off for your benefit, but it will also benefit your family, friends, and clients. Your rested self will return refreshed and ready to cope with the new workload — without the old feelings of stress and exhaustion.

When you do take a break, make sure that it's a break. You might want to put your out-of-office on, log out from social media, maybe even delete a few apps for the time you're away. It can feel like you're letting go of the reins, but in fact, you'll be gaining control of your mind and your time, helping to bring you more fully into the present.

Make sure you're using micro-pockets of time to recharge your energy. From midday snoozes to power naps, help your body to stay on track and in tune with Circadian rhythms and energy flow. Listen to your body. Both it and your mind will thank you in the long run

Learn to say 'no'

A corollary of daring to set your auto-reply to 'out of office' is learning to say no. You might be all set for a day off when a client rings wanting something. In that instant, it can feel like turning them down will end your career, but the likelihood is that it won't, and if they do get funny about it, then they're probably not the kind of client who has anyone's well-being on their list of priorities.

Similarly, a client might want to set an unrealistic deadline, and you have the power to say 'no' in a positive way by offering an alternative deadline and explaining why it's more realistic. Some of you may feel tense just reading this, thinking, "But surely they'll just get someone else to do it?" However, the thing to remember is that they've come to you, and if they've done that, then they believe you're the person for the job. Obviously, context matters (if a current news item has to be written that day, then completing it a week hence isn't going to be reasonable), but generally speaking, you'll be surprised how flexible and adaptable people can be when a) you're good at what you do and b) you say "no, but" in a constructive way.

The less-surprising outcome of setting these kinds of boundaries and choosing what's right for you should never be underestimated: the ability to say no to things that don't feel quite right, to follow your heart and gut feeling, and to act in your own best interests. This isn't a blank cheque to turn down all that comes your way; it's the antidote to saying yes to everything out of fear. If an opportunity doesn't excite you enough, then you should know what to do next. Say no.

Smile on the inside

Throughout all of this, through all of the ups and downs and tedious middles, something that might sound a bit whimsical (even cheesy) but which can really help, is to find time and reason to smile and laugh. Not in a bitter, cynical, or mocking way, but because you find something funny or because you're happy.

Finding something smile-worthy every day can help put

things into perspective and fight negative thought patterns. And modern life can easily become overly serious, especially if we're working on stuff alone. True, we have the same memes and reels flying past our eyes every day, but we've probably seen them all before, and if we're scrolling, we're likely not concentrating.

Whether you can make the time to watch a favourite comedy, laugh with mates in person or in a WhatsApp group, or even Google the worst dad jokes going, keeping a sense of humour when all around are losing theirs is a valuable life skill. What's more, like yawning, laughter is contagious, and so if you're around others, a good laugh can help lift the mood (leading us back to the mood-action cycle)

Keeping positive habits

The accumulation of positive habits will add up and yield a return, making future days, work, and partnerships easier and more enjoyable. The constant and often cringe-worthy advertising product copy about tomorrow starting today is actually true. It's all about the work we put in. If you don't keep hold of your day, then someone else will take control — and that could be anyone from an overly demanding boss to soft-drinks manufacturers that have you craving their products. The same applies to your mind and wellbeing. Once again, own it.

The final thing to say is that this is an ongoing process. There is always something new to learn and a new way of seeing things. There are new technologies and new approaches; there's new research and new ways of thinking. As you grow and practise positive habits that work for you, then you can uncover new things about yourself. Being open to this can help you to maintain command over your day, and therefore your life.

"Creativity is a habit, and the best creativity is the result of good work habits."

Twyla Tharp

Pages

186–203

Section - no.8

Flow states

Chapter - no.8

What do we expect from creativity?

It's a simple question, but it's one that even the most self-analytical creatives might never have thought to ask themselves. What do we expect from our creativity? Yes, we expect it will help us to generate good ideas and realise the things our imagination comes up with, but what do we expect it to do for us? Do we want it to make us feel happy? Satisfied? Energised? Calm? And when do we expect that to happen? At the beginning, middle, or end of the process?

Whatever your answer, it's likely that it can be found when you get into a state of flow.

Flow States

A flow state is that period of pure focus when your creativity flows. You're in the moment, the ideas are coming, you feel in control, you're pushing against the walls of your comfort zone, time becomes meaningless, and any other bullshit has been put to one side. It's a state that has always existed but which was systemised by a Hungarian-American psychologist called Mihalyi Csikszentmihalyi in the late 20th century. His studies led him to the belief that we are at our happiest, most creative, and most satisfied when we are in a state of flow. It's an active state with, according to Csikzentmilhalyi, eight characteristics:

1. — Complete concentration on the task in hand.
2. — Clear goals, a reward, and immediate feedback.
3. — A sense of either having all the time in the world or time flying by.
4. — The task is immensely rewarding.
5. — The work feels easy and effortless, but not in a boring way.
6. — The right balance of using your skills and being challenged.
7. — Action and awareness becoming one; no ruminating.
8. — Feeling in control of the task.

Flow states are different to mindfulness. You can be totally mindful but still stuck in the middle of unproductive chaos — the difference is that you're now aware that you're stuck in the middle of unproductive chaos. For creatives, flow states are the next step along from mindfulness; they're far more active. You do, not just observe.

Like mindfulness, however, flow states don't appear out of nowhere, and they generally can't be willed into being if the conditions aren't right. As ever, you are the gardener, creating the optimal conditions for flow states to grow. And this takes commitment and effort

Give a shit

Think of a dancer performing a routine at the very peak of their powers: the lightness, the grace, the seemingly effortless flow. And then think of everything that will have gone into making that magic moment happen. If we want to get the most out of our creative process, both to do our best work and get maximum personal fulfilment, then we have to adopt the same kind of overall approach.

Generating and maintaining the optimal conditions won't necessarily lead to a flow state, but not generating or maintaining them gives you far less chance. You're also unlikely to get into a flow state by doing something you don't care about or that is lacking in one or more of the eight characteristics described above. If a task doesn't challenge you, is overly challenging, has an insufficient reward, or is just not your cup of tea, then it's far more likely to be a slog; you're more likely to procrastinate, become distracted, or phone it in. In short, it doesn't happen by accident; you have to push yourself and you have to give a shit about what you're doing

How to get into the flow

There are plenty of practical things you can do to not necessarily induce a flow state, but certainly to shorten the odds on hitting one and being able to fully embrace it:

Set your goals. If you don't know where you're going, you'll never get there. This is where it helps to know your brief, break it down into smaller, logical steps; and aim to achieve what is manageable given your circumstances (i.e., unless you're very confident in your ability to thrive under pressure — and love doing so — then don't leave a week's worth of work until Friday lunchtime).

Get rid of distractions. This step sounds obvious, but in our increasingly distraction-filled world, our dopamine receptors can very subtly, and sometimes very slyly, take our minds away from our creative process. If you're settling down to some creative work, then log out of your social media accounts (or even delete the apps; they only take a few seconds to reinstall later on), put your phone on 'do not disturb', tell anyone else around that you're going to be working, and either create a quiet environment, or if music helps, stick something on. You can even do a brief meditation or yoga practice for focus before you start. The key is to be in the best position to dive into your work and fully immerse yourself in it. If you've ever felt so deeply involved in a creative task that you've almost needed time to readjust to the real world afterwards, then you know what you're aiming for.

Have a routine and keep to it. As much as flow states can feel like magic, especially when they take us out of clock time and make all the other stuff going on around us seem unimportant, they're more likely to appear when you take solid actions like showing up regularly. If you clock in and make the effort time after time, you'll be training your mind in the habit of creativity. From there, you're far closer to a flow state than you are when you're showing up sporadically and half-heartedly.

Do a warm-up task. Before embarking on a project or a day's work, it can help to loosen up the creative muscle by doing a warm-up exercise. This could be something as seemingly trivial as doodling or a little bit of automatic writing. It's the equivalent of a musician tuning their instrument and playing a few scales or favourite riffs to get their fingers warmed up.

Set your time. If you want to hit a flow state, then make sure you've got enough time to do so. If you've made the effort to get your optimal conditions just right, then you don't want to find you only have five minutes left before you have to go and fetch the kids or a similar life task. Likewise, keep your time allotted in manageable chunks. Planning to work from dawn 'til dusk without a break won't heighten your chances of hitting a state of flow; it'll wear you out.

Push yourself a little. Challenge yourself to go beyond the edges of your comfort zone. Remember, states of flow occur when we respond to challenges that we're not used to but are equal to. If you've got your various positive habits instilled, then you'll have the strength and confidence to go further than you have before.

By implementing these simple rules and tasks around your creative practice, you'll be creating the optimal conditions for both growth and depth.

The benefits of flow states

The personal benefits that can come from flow states, and from working to reach them regularly, are many. For a start, adopting the above strategies can enhance your working day by removing any self-laid blocks that are in your way. This can benefit your mental health by placing you in a space where you are more likely to be calm, focused, and happy. And as well as the physical achievement of (probably) getting a lot more work done, there will be the inner sense of achievement from upping and optimising your game. The quality of your work can improve, and you're less likely to come away from it feeling dissatisfied or as if you've somehow wasted your time.

To top it all, flow states can be incredibly liberating. They're times when your mind is on the ball and not being dragged into all kinds of touchline distractions and ruminations. You're focused on a specific goal and you're taking logical, productive steps to get there whilst simultaneously staying open to the magic of your creative superpowers. It's a balance beam that you can stride confidently along, and maybe even do a few cartwheels along for good measure.

Flow states are our play, our time to tune into ourselves, channel our experience and influences, and unlock the deep potential within us

The importance of Beginner's Mind

We've talked a lot about plans and goals and routines, but as intimated above, there always has to be a healthy balance. Like anyone working to attain a state that relies on a combination of commitment, routine, and some near-magical elements (think of anyone from a ballet dancer to a fisherman), we can box ourselves in without realising. If we become too narrowly focused on a fixed result or assumption, then it can become counterproductive. We can't lose ourselves in the flow of our creativity because we're constantly measuring it against a rigid idea of what we want to achieve. It can even become dangerous when we can't let go — some genius musicians have run themselves off a mental cliff trying to recreate the sound they hear in their heads.

A highly useful way of countering this kind of rigidity when looking to generate flow states is Beginner's Mind. It's a concept that comes from Zen Buddhism, where it is known as Shoshin. In essence, it means looking at everything with the same level of openness, excitement, and curiosity as when we were first exposed to it. Think back, and I'm sure most of you can remember when you first discovered the joy of your own creative discipline, how whole worlds suddenly opened up before you, and how you couldn't wait to learn more, to practise, and to learn the next new part of the process. Beginner's Mind is that beautiful moment, but brought to every new brief or piece of work. Of course, it's easier said than done, especially when you've been doing what you do for a long time, but when looking to initiate flow states, Beginner's Mind can ground you in the present moment whilst simultaneously keeping you open to the potential of your creative power.

If we work to stay aware and open as to what we can achieve within any required parameters, then we cultivate the right conditions for the more magical elements of the creative flow: where fresh ideas seem to spring from nowhere, allowing us to go beyond anything we've achieved before, and feeling comfortable and confident in doing so.

Invest in your space

We've talked about creative space in a kind of spiritual way so far, but reaching that space requires the optimal physical space to work in too. Working from home has become much more prevalent in creative industries, and has long been the natural territory of the freelancer. But when we're working from the sofa or our bed, comfortable though it may be, are we putting ourselves in the best position to work undistracted and unhindered, and to tap into that flow state?

I would argue that your living space and your office should

enticing magic and part of why we yearn for the time and space to create — because today might be the day that the idea that's been niggling at us for a few days turns into the best thing we've ever created. We might even come up with something brilliant out of thin air.

When it's not happening, look back to some of the previous steps in this book. Find a moment to search for clarity and uncover any obstacles that might be in the way. Use mindful acceptance and observation to step away and return to your work later.

Life will always throw things in the way too. It won't do it maliciously or deliberately; that's just how things work once you're an adult with responsibilities. You might have children to look after, relationships to tend to and nurture, shopping to fetch, food to cook, the desperate desire to just sit down with a cup of tea for five minutes — the hundreds of things that fill up the hours when you're neither working nor asleep.

And sometimes, yes, it can feel like the whole world is conspiring to keep you from your art, but if it's truly what you want to do and you consistently set out to achieve the optimal conditions for getting into that creative flow, then you will find the time and space with surprising ease.

"The gardener does not make a plant grow. The job of a gardener is to create optimal conditions."

Ken Robinson

Pages

204–221

Chapter - no.9

Grow

ONE WAY

You are your work in progress

Every section of this book points to the same end: your continual growth as a creative human being. Growth never stops if you don't want it to, but it can easily splutter and come to a standstill if you don't keep your cup topped up — i.e., if you fall (back) into unhelpful, negative habits. There is no finished 'you'; the work doesn't stop when the immediate pain goes away. Life, creative or otherwise, is a constant series of small efforts that all have their part to play in the overall picture.

Once you've got your positive habits and routines up and running, it's vital that you keep them in place and continue to work at them. They will become more like second-nature over time, but it's surprising how easy we can lapse back into negative habits, especially when something beyond our control throws us off-course.

For example, you might make the effort to exercise every day and then get injured and be unable to perform your usual routine.

We can usually find some alternative way to get our exercise in, but we can just as easily become discouraged and quickly get used to not exercising again. It can require a conscious effort to get back on it. You need self-discipline to keep yourself on track and motivated.

For growth to continue, we have to keep learning, about ourselves and the world and the people around us. In order to learn, we have to remain open, receptive, and humble; we have to make mistakes every now and again, and even embrace failure. Of course, when mistakes occur and failure happens all the old negative thought patterns and habits will be waiting in a darkened corner of your mind, like an unwanted surprise party. Occasionally, you may slip back, but you will always remember to get back up, and you will always have a little more knowledge than you did before.

Learn, do, and share

When we find something that truly enriches our lives — a piece of music, a book, a recipe, a new band or artist, yoga, meditation, journaling, etc. — we can become a missionary for it, sending links to our friends, sharing it on our socials, telling anyone we think will benefit — telling anyone who'll listen — about our brilliant new discovery. Sometimes it can work, and we can open doors for people who might only have seen a wall in front of them. And of course, if we keep our antennae up, other people can do the same for us.

We can also be of service to others when we share our

experiences, both positive and negative. When we do this from a place of authenticity, then it benefits us and them equally — if we're struggling with something, sharing can offload some of the personal heaviness we feel — and of course, it can benefit others who might be going through the same or similar things.

Doing this can help us to dial up our empathy and compassion because we can realise that, even if we're at different stages of our journeys, we're all more connected than we realise. We can learn to suspend the quick judgements and jealousies that social media encourages and see that in our different ways, we're all trying to make it and we're all doing the best we can with what we have at the time.

As we become more conscious of ourselves and others, we can also learn to spot when someone needs a nudge or a lift or just someone to listen. And we don't just have to be there for the trying times either; we can become cheerleaders for others as well as ourselves. If we see someone enjoying success in our chosen field, then rather than wail, "But what about me?!" or feel like that person is somehow stealing success from us, then we do have the choice to be happy for them and to celebrate their win. Obviously, that might be a little more difficult to do if they narrowly beat you to a lucrative contract, but 99 times out of 100, their success will be in something that doesn't negatively affect you. In fact, it might end up being beneficial to you, too.

A valuable counterweight to this is learning when and where your energy is being drained. Our passion for the actions and habits that have enriched our lives can sometimes make us a little naïve — we think that they will instantly do the same for everyone and that everyone will be motivated to do them. However, if you see a friend, colleague, or loved one struggling and they're unwilling to at least try and help themselves, or even recognise that something's not right, then no amount of sharing, suggesting, or cheerleading will help. As we know from our own experiences, meaningful change can only come from within. Trying to help someone who doesn't want help is as much of a waste of your time and energy as arguing with strangers in the comments section of your local newspaper's Facebook page.

Likewise, we can find ourselves becoming drained by working for clients who don't pay us properly, keep asking us for extra work, or contact us at unsociable hours, expecting us to jump at their command. If they double down on their behaviour when constructively challenged, then no amount of positive language can dress up the fact that we probably shouldn't be working for them. Part of learning, sharing, and doing is recognising and cherishing your worth and ensuring (in a positive way) that others know and respect it.

Making and recording your progress

Although we always want to keep growing and moving forwards, pausing to glance over our shoulder and reflect on how far we've come can be an essential part of that progress — as can keeping a record of that progress in a journal.

Journaling is a great way of remembering the high and lows, the lessons, and the positive and poignant moments of life. Even small notes scribbled at the end of each day can help you in multiple ways. It encourages you to actively reflect on your day, it can help to put things in perspective and perhaps ease the impact of stress, and it's a small but strong habit to build as you learn and grow.

Journals are for nobody's eyes but yours if you don't want them to be — you're not writing a status for all to see and comment on. There's no 'right' way to journal, and it doesn't have to be crammed with positives to be worthwhile; it's there for the good, bad, and the mundane. If there are times when it feels like you're clutching at straws trying to find positives or you're in a period where it feels like only negative stuff is happening, then don't beat yourself up about it, and most importantly, don't let your journaling habit lapse.

Another way of marking your progress is to get yourself a 'progress buddy'. This could be a peer, a mate, a spouse, a sibling, anyone that you trust to be honest and constructive. The aim is to encourage each other and to hold each other accountable where progress is concerned.

Again, this doesn't need to be a major event in your life, but if you've got someone that you can regularly check-in with, sharing the goods and not-so-goods of each other's progress, then it can work wonders for both of you because there's somebody there who, in a friendly and supportive way, is going to hold you accountable for how you're spending your time and energy. It can encourage your empathy and compassion too — if your buddy is struggling with something, it's unlikely that you'll want to do anything other than reassure them that everything will be okay.

It cannot be overstated that all of this is best done at your own pace. It takes as long as it takes for you. Yes, some people will (appear to) progress faster than you. They may share pictures of journals filled with elaborate writing and decoration, whereas you secretly scribble a sentence or two into a tattered notebook every evening, but that's okay; this isn't school. You're not going to get marked down for presentation or not writing enough. What matters is nurturing your consistency, your ability to reflect, and your ability to act positively on your reflections.

Keeping the past in the past

It's helpful to glance over your shoulder and see how far you've come, but as anyone who's changed lanes on a motorway will tell you, that's all you need: a glance backwards, and then back to what's in front of you.

We can never go back to the past. If we've had times when we've really fucked up, be it in work, relationships, or damaging ourselves through unhealthy behaviour and vices, then we can't change it or deny it. But we can own it, learn from it, make amends if need be, and then make peace with it. And if that's all we can possibly do, then that's enough. Ignore anyone who demands people are forever judged by mistakes that they have held themselves accountable for. It's okay to make mistakes, and it's pointless to keep beating ourselves up over them. That's not progress or growth; that's standing, looking backwards, staring at the past and letting the potential of the future pass you by. You can only heal by moving on.

When we do start to become entranced by the past, or even

when we think we're totally clear of it, then old bad habits can start to creep in. Many is the smoker who has successfully quit only to fool themselves that they can have one cigarette to prove that they're no longer addicted (if you've never smoked, that may sound ridiculous; but if you have, then you'll appreciate the warped logic). Get wise to yourself and any old addictive habits you have; learn to spot when healthy habits are starting to slide, and above all, be honest with yourself about what you're consuming. If you can kid yourself that, say, the hour you spend every day playing Candy Crush Saga is good for you, then that's your loss and nobody else's.

Keep coming back to the strategies and actions outlined in this book, and review your progress regularly. Celebrate your wins and acknowledge where there's still work to be done. And don't be afraid to make mistakes. It's a fact of life that you will make them and fall on your arse every now and again. But each time you do, as long as you keep doing the work, you'll be able to get up and dust yourself off more quickly than the previous time

The power of gratitude and affirmations

We may have different ideas about how and why we're here and doing the job that we do, but whatever our thoughts, I believe that we should celebrate our moment in the sun, however long or fleeting it may be. Having gratitude for the big and small things in our lives can have a powerful effect on how we see the world, and by extension, how we see ourselves.

We can show gratitude in subtle ways. For example, when

we're working on our creative business, we can frame it as "I get to work on this project", not "I have to do this work". There's an element of perception equalling reality, but it does help us to take stock and remember that every day that we're not in a need-to-work situation — working in a service job that we hate and have no interest in (but have to pretend we do), all whilst having to wear a demeaning uniform — is a win for us. We get to do the creative work. And in our own business, we can have a greater say over our present and our future.

Sometimes, doing the opposite — seeing everything as crap and pointless — can be really easy. It can even feel comforting sometimes, especially if that's how you've viewed the world for many years. But relentless negativity gives us nothing, and as you start practising gratitude for the good things in your life, you'll quickly notice when people are excessively negative and self-deprecating, and it'll become off-putting. If you've been the kind to crack nasty jokes at your own or others' expense, then you'll soon stop finding that kind of dark, cynical humour funny; you'll realise that it comes from a place of insecurity and unhappiness, of seeing the world and everyone in it as a potential threat, not as a source of growth and learning.

We can show gratitude in how we talk to ourselves and to others. We can give compliments and encouragements freely. We can also receive them without giving in to the urge to qualify them by saying, "Oh, it's not that good. Anyone could have done it, really." We can reply to negative emails positively and constructively. We can use positive affirmations ("I am...", "I have...", "I get to...", "I choose to...") to build our self-worth.

We can also extend this to what we don't say or do. In the same way that we can save wasting our time and energy on people who don't want it, we can choose not to get involved in negative online conversations that, to be brutally honest, won't change anyone's mind about anything and only serve to give us a self-righteous hit of dopamine — I'm talking about Twitter/X pile-ons, commenting on outrage-generating clickbait, shaming and judging others, rage-posting, arguing with strangers, and sharing endless angry political content. You don't have to become passive, unrealistically happy, or ignorant to what's going on in the world, but putting ceaseless negative energy out there will likely only bring you more negative energy. It's a basic algorithm. And it won't fill your cup.

A headwind is always guaranteed

As creatives, we're always going to spend at least half of our journey cycling into a headwind — we're always going to face challenges. And although some challenges can be more testing than others, that's ultimately a good thing. We're hardwired to need challenges. If we're never challenged, we never learn and we settle down in our comfortable little rut. We get bored and resentful and we fall into bad habits. We need to be inspired to take action, because no action equals no reward. Nothing comes of nothing.

It can also be beneficial for us to challenge ourselves from time to time — and please note that there's a difference between challenging yourself and shoving a stick into your own spokes.

There's also a difference between challenging yourself to raise your game and judging yourself against impossibly high standards. The healthy kinds of growth-oriented habit-building challenges you can set yourself include challenging yourself to perform a certain task (such as journaling or exercise or meditation) every day for a set period of time, even if it means waking up a little earlier.

You might challenge yourself to start learning something new, such as a language or an instrument or a craft like woodwork or crochet. You might push yourself out of your comfort zone by joining a local group of some kind (sports, amateur dramatics, etc.), or if you're a musician, performing at an open mic night.

Whichever way you challenge yourself, it'll likely feel a little uncomfortable, but that's good because if it feels totally comfortable, then you're definitely not learning anything. Of course, there are those magic moments when you challenge yourself to do something new and you instantly feel as though you've been doing it all your life, but generally, your feet will have to leave the ground for you to step up.

Don't give up

We can all think of times in our lives when we've just wanted to give up and go home, to take the easy route. There are times when it's been because we're in totally the wrong situation for us, and there are times when we've walked away and regretted it. There are also doubtless times when we persisted and ended up glad we did.

I was once cycling up a mountain on the Greek Island of

Rhodes, already tired from a lack of sleep the night before. I was falling behind the group I was with, and my legs were screaming at me to stop, turn around, and roll back down. But my curiosity as to what was on the other side of the mountain kept me going. It took longer than I would've liked, but I got there, and as I sailed down the other side, the endorphins kicked in, and I realised just how hard I'd worked to get up that mountain. The sense of achievement after was worth the pain of the climb (it also reminded me about being a parent to young children who never sleep through the night).

Sometimes, we can think we have everything in place and things still won't add up, it'll feel like we're on a false flat — a path that appears level but is actually slightly uphill — and those are times when we might end up questioning ourselves and wondering whether the problem lies with us, whether we're strong enough. But the more you do the habits outlined in this book, the stronger and better prepared you will be to identify those kinds of challenges and rise to them. You will know yourself and your capabilities better; you will accept where you're at but remain excited about what's on the other side of the mountain.

You and your creativity are worth investing your time, energy, and love in. You might not (yet) have reached the heights you dreamed of reaching when you first started; you might not have built the audience, reputation, or financial stability that your peers built in a seemingly very short space of time, but you can only be where you are, and you can only be you, with your unique talents and ideas.

The reason this book exists is because I don't want you to give up on your growth as a creative. You might fall off every now and again, but you can always get back on the bike and start pedalling again. That extra little push to keep going and to try again might be the one that ends up changing your life in ways you never dreamed of.

I believe we don't have to ponder whether the glass is half full or half empty. We can celebrate the fact we have a glass in the first place. Fill it up to where it makes you enjoy what's inside.

Bonus Content

Visit **brandnubooks.co.uk** to access *Mindful Creative* bonus content, including audio meditation files, suggested reading list, image downloads, playlist links and more.

Also available by Radim Malinic

Book of Ideas - Vol.1 - a journal of creative direction and graphic design / ISBN 978-0-9935400-0-4
Book of Ideas - Vol.2 - a journal of creative direction and graphic design / ISBN 978-0-9935400-1-1
Book of Branding - a guide to creating brand identity or startups and beyond / ISBN 978-0-9935400-3-5
Pause, Breathe and Grow - notes on mindful creative life ISBN 978-0-9935400-2-8
Creativity For Sale - how to start and grow a life-changing creative career and business / ISBN 978-0-9935400-4-2
All titles are available in paperpack and kindle format
brandnubooks.co.uk

"Don't go through life, grow through life."

Eric Butterworth